When my father, George Verity, shipped out to the Philippine Islands in 1941 he was an agnostic. His father quit going to church after the KKK grand wizard and several other hooded men marched down the aisle of the Methodist Church in McLoud, Oklahoma and gave the minister a contribution (which was warmly received). After making the Bataan Death March, Dad lay sick and dying of bari bari, malaria, acute malnutrition and diarrhea at Zinsuji POW camp in Japan. He had been triaged to the area for those too sick to help and left for dead. At his wits end and being helpless he recited what he called the agnostic's prayer – God if you are there please help me. In a matter of minutes he had an acute sense of warmth and light. In a matter of days he was sitting up and shortly thereafter walked back to the main camp a changed man. During the rest of his POW days he did whatever he could to learn about the God that had healed him. He began to pray for guards who miraculously then were in turn kind to him. In this process he found and read "I Will Lift Up Mine Eyes" by Glen Clark. The book meant so much to him that he frequently bought the book and gave it away. Finally he couldn't get any more because the book was out of print. Not to be deterred he went to the publisher and bought a whole run. After Dad's death my brothers and I still have about 350 copies of this book. We want to make as many of the books as possible available to those of you who might find a use for them at one of your camps.

D1246552

I WILL LIFT
UP MINE EYES

I WILL LIFT UP MINE EYES

A step-by-step guide to spiritual growth

By

GLENN CLARK

Special Edition
for George L. Verity

1817

HARPER & ROW, PUBLISHERS, SAN FRANCISCO

Cambridge, Hagerstown, New York, Philadelphia
London, Mexico City, São Paulo, Singapore, Sydney

FIRST PAPERBACK EDITION

Design by Richard Gorsuch

Library of Congress Cataloging in Publication Data

Clark, Glenn, 1882–1956.
    I WILL LIFT UP MINE EYES.

    1. Prayer. 2. Lord's Prayer. I. Title.
[BV210.C54   1984]   248.3'2   77-7830
ISBN 0-06-061394-7 (pbk.)

---

84 85 86 87 88 10 9 8 7 6 5 4 3 2 1

Contents

I WILL LIFT
UP MINE EYES

Hind's Feet That Lead to High Places

I was sitting alone in a little restaurant waiting for someone to take my order, and looking absentmindedly out of the window. I felt an inner turmoil, and the whirling wind and the pattering rain outside did not do much to allay my mood. Just then the door opened and in came Dan McArthur.

McArthur was a vigorous young cleric, struggling along in some little out-of-the-way church, a happy-go-lucky, likable chap, the kind one usually expects to go so far and no farther in any field he enters. I had known him in college days. I sprang a little wisecrack about winds bringing breezy guests, but he did not answer me in the old bantering tones. Instead, as he sat down opposite me and reached his hand across, clasping mine with a firm grip, I was aware of a strange new power in his presence. It stirred something in me to the very marrow of my bones. As I looked into his eyes his whole countenance fairly shone.

I asked him what he would have, and after scanning the menu carefully he ordered from it leisurely, and invited me to join him in luncheon for two. I assented, wondering at the indomitable something about him, an atmosphere of dignity and power—well, I guess you would call it self-unconsciousness—that I had never noted before.

"What has happened to you?" I finally blurted out. "Have you inherited a million dollars?"

"Greater than that," he smiled, "I have found the water of life."

"Ponce de Leon or monkey glands?" I inquired.

"I see that I have surprised you," he said, putting his coffee-cup away from his lips. "It is not strange, for I am a surprise to myself. I am a new man, and the alteration has taken place within the last six months. I wouldn't change places with a millionaire."

"You wouldn't!" I exclaimed, incredulously, for I had always thought that Dan liked money. "No," he said, buttering his roll. "A millionaire has spent his enthusiasm; mine is all at hand."

"You amaze me," I replied, wondering if he had been drinking wine. "Won't you tell me your secret? I should like to hear it."

"It is very simple," he said smiling. "All you have to do is to make your feet like hind's feet and God will do the rest."

"Hind's feet!" I exclaimed, "Hind's feet! I don't get the idea. Will you explain?"

"Gladly. I intend to tell the whole world. A few months ago I was in what I thought was a blind alley. I thought that nothing on sea or land could take me out of it. I was in a rut, inside and out. Then out of the blue sky I heard a story. I was on a train between Boston and Portland when I met a white-haired gentleman who talked with me one hour. Just one hour, mind you, but that one hour changed me inside and outside. It would have changed you, too. You have no idea what it did for me. Nothing is impossible after that story. It makes everything as plain as A-B-C."

"How can a story work such wonders?" I gasped.

"Very simple. Listen. First something happens inside one. Get that? *Inside* one—deep, deep down inside one. Secretly, silently, invisibly inside one. Understand?"

"Yes," I said.

"Then—and here is the strange part of it—here is the miraculous part that you will find hard to believe—after the change happens *inside*, everything begins to change *outside*, too."

"I don't believe I see the logic," I replied. "I don't see the connection."

"Never mind; you will—as soon as you hear the story. That is, as soon as you hear it and practice it. Practicing it is very important."

"What has it done for you?" I asked. "What has it brought you on the outside? I can see by looking into your eyes that it has brought you something on the inside."

His eyes shone like stars at this compliment. "You know what a little job I had before," he replied. "Well, that wasn't what bothered me. What hurt me was the knowledge that I wasn't adequate for that job, much less something greater. After that hour on the train I began for the first time to render real service to my people. Then out of a clear sky I was called to one of the greatest churches in the United States," and he named a church which I considered, in some ways, the most famous church in America.

"Just to think," I exclaimed, "that you are now an assistant pastor in the greatest church in America!"

"Not assistant pastor," he corrected, "but head pastor."

"What!" I exclaimed, no longer able to hide my amazement. "I can't believe it."

He smiled, not at all provoked by my unabashed incredulity. "You see, it works."

"It must be a remarkable story!" I cried, now my curiosity fully aroused. "Please tell it to me."

"All right, I will tell you, though really you should hear it from the old gentleman himself. However, I will tell you the best I can. It is like this. You see ——"

The waiter interrupted us at that moment, saying that some one on the phone wanted "Reverend Dan McArthur." "Pardon me," he said. "I'll be right back," and he hurried away. Soon he returned, saying, "Sorry, but an unexpected call demands my instant attention," and he rushed out.

Some months later I was in New York City, walking down Broadway. At the corner of Twenty-third I met my friend Joe Benson in the middle of the crowded street. He must have been watching me for some time. His eyes had evidently been smiling at me in the kindliest way before I saw him. I had never thought of Joe as an especially "benevolent old gentleman," but he certainly was the picture of it now. Joe, though undoubtedly possessed of real talent, had never gotten his talent across. But there was something very majestic and sweeping and all-conquering about him as he approached me, smiling, that day. As he reached out and shook my hand I felt a thrill clear through me, to the center of my being. He looked squarely into my eyes and his countenance fairly shone. There was an air of dignity and power and—yes, unencumbered unself-consciousness—about him that could not be concealed.

"Still playing in the town band?" I asked.

"Come in here," he said, drawing me into a drug store.

"I have a lot to tell you."

"Lemonade for two," he ordered, and drew me to a side table. "You used to be a teetotaler." He turned to me in inquiry.

"Righto," I smiled. "And still am."

"What have you heard about me?" he asked as he sipped through a straw. I hate straws. I drank mine down at two gulps. It was a hot day.

"I heard that you had applied for a job with a famous orchestra and had been turned down."

"Right," he exclaimed with a laugh. "But did you hear the sequel?" I shook my head. "Well, it was this way," he continued. "I was riding out of New York, on the New Haven and Hartford, when a white-haired gentleman sat down beside me. He turned to me and without a moment's hesitation said, 'You are discouraged, young man, and you have no right to be.' I replied that I thought I had a right to be, after spending time and toil and money for years and years in the most careful, thorough preparation, only to find that every door was closed against me. He smiled very pleasantly and said, 'Change your feet to hind's feet, young man, and your luck will change.' "

"Hind's feet!" I exclaimed, startled. "Go on. Tell me the rest. What happened?"

"Well, I went on to my destination and didn't pay much attention to what the old man had said. Then a few weeks later in the middle of the night I awoke and suddenly realized what he meant. I took the first train to New York, went straight back to the same company—yes, the same company that had turned me down, and asked them if there was a chance for me to have a small part and show them what I could do. The director asked

me point blank if I could play the 'cello in a famous com-
position which he named. I said, 'Yes.' He replied, 'Our
leading 'cellist has just this hour been stricken with a se-
vere illness. He will be out for two months. You are to
take his place.' 'When do I start?' I cried, hardly believing
my ears. 'Tomorrow night.' I almost fainted."

"I'll swear that if I hadn't seen you drink lemonade—"
I began. His laugh interrupted me. "But the hind's feet!"
I exclaimed. "Tell me what they had to do with it."

"It's a long story," he replied, "and as I am expecting a
long-distance call in a few minutes, I'll have to ask you to
come with me to the company's office right away. It is
just across the street. I'll tell you on the way."

The din of traffic in a great New York street drowned
our conversation until we entered a high building. Then
Joe turned to me, "When you get hind's feet you learn
first of all that you must get quiet inside—deep, deep
down inside. Do you catch on?"

We had now entered the elevator. "But how does the
change happen inside?" I asked. "That is what I want to
know."

"That is where the secret lies. But here we are."

As we entered the rooms a secretary rushed in to meet
him. "So glad you are here, Mr. Benson. They have been
trying for an hour to get you on the long-distance from
Detroit. They want you to be the 'cello soloist tomorrow
night, and the train leaves right away."

"Sorry, old chap," he said to me, "but I must go. Come
in again some other time when I have a lot of leisure, and
I'll try to tell you the whole thing from beginning to end."

I returned to Chicago on one of those windy, gusty
days when all Lake Michigan seemed blowing down

across the streets. As the little college in Illinois where I was going to resume my second year of teaching would not open for a few days, I decided that I would attend some lecture or play or concert that night, and resume my journey on the morrow. Finding by the papers that Miss Marian Graw, author of a best-selling novel, would lecture that evening at a well-known lecture-hall, I made my plans to attend.

It was a very interesting lecture, but it was not till near the very close that the startling thing happened. Suddenly she came to the front of the platform and said, "Now I am going to tell you how I came to write this book. I had gone to Colorado as a broken-down school-teacher, without any money and without any friends, and threatened with tuberculosis. I tried my hand at writing, but without success. Then one day while riding on the train between Greeley and Denver I met a white-haired man who told me I should cease living in the lowlands of life, and travel on hind's feet to the high places. I took his advice and changed myself from a factory, trying to manufacture ideas, into a channel for letting ideas flow through me. And this book—this best seller—is the result."

She stopped speaking and I pressed my way to the platform, but before I could get there she was gone. She was on the way to the train, I was told, to meet her next lecture engagement.

The following day I resumed my journey to the college town where I was to continue my career as a teacher of creative writing and reading. Three months later, on a cold December day, I was riding between Aledo, Illinois, and Des Moines, Iowa, on my way home for the Christmas holidays. The big event of the holidays was to be my wedding.

I was looking out of the window at the snowflakes whisking down when I noticed an elderly man, with white hair, walking slowly through the car, looking in a benign way into the countenances of the passengers as he went by. When he reached my seat he halted.

"Pardon me," he said, "but would you mind if I sat down in the seat beside you for a while?"

"Certainly not," I replied. As soon as he was seated he turned to me. "You are engaged in religious work of some kind, are you not?" he asked.

"Oh no," I answered, laughing. "I am merely a teacher of literature and a coach of athletics."

He hesitated for just a moment. "But you have a spiritual influence upon the young men you associate with, do you not?"

I hesitated. "Well, perhaps I do."

"I am in a business," he began, "that carries me to all parts of the country. On every journey I find myself led to tell my story to one person. God always directs me to the person to whom I am to tell it, and now I find myself led to tell it to you."

"I shall be glad to hear your story," I replied.

"It happened to me in this wise. I had come to Akron, Ohio, as a young man of energy and promise. I threw myself headlong into my business and it began to thrive beyond all expectations. I was soon head of the firm. Not satisfied with being president of one concern, I organized another, and then became director of others. I was making money hand over fist. All I thought about, morning, noon, and night, was money, money, money. And then something happened. It always happens when you burn the candle at both ends and leave God out of the picture, doesn't it? I had a breakdown.

"Well, the doctor said I was done with, that my working-days were over, my only hope lay in making some drastic changes in my life. He told me to go to a lake and rest—do nothing but rest for months and months. Then he would see if I could do any work again.

"I went to Isle Royal in Lake Superior. As my strength gradually returned I would go out in a rowboat and idle about for hours. Something about the wide expanse of water beneath a summer sky rested me—it was doing something to me inside and outside. A new peace began to enter into me. And then the great experience happened.

"I had gone out in a boat, near sunset. I was rather drowsy and before I knew it I had fallen asleep. When I awoke hours later the boat was out of sight of land, and there was no way for me to determine whether I was north, south, or east of the island. Knowing how quickly a squall can arise on Lake Superior and how easily a boat is overturned, also how drowned bodies never come to the surface in this coldest of all northern waters, I was filled with a panic of fear. I started to pray, and then found that I couldn't. And why? Simply because I wasn't worthy to pray. My whole past came up before me. What would be the value of saving a man like me, a man who did nothing but accumulate money for himself? What would the world lose if I should never return?

"And then I made a promise to God. I promised Him that if He would save me I would devote half of my time henceforth to His work, to helping mankind, especially young people. And then the answer came."

At this point the old gentleman fumbled in his pocket and brought forth a picture postal card. It looked exactly like a photograph. It was a pictorial arrangement of a man alone in a rowboat on a lake, and above his head were the moon and stars, and among the stars one immense star—about ten times the size of the other stars, and about one-fourth the size of the moon. I wondered if the Star of Bethlehem could have looked like that.

"This star suddenly appeared in the sky," he said, pointing to the large star in the picture. "It was an immense star, such as I had never seen before. I was overwhelmed with the mystery and wonder of it, but taking it as a sign I fixed my eyes upon it and, keeping it at the tail of my boat, I rowed and rowed without looking around for hours and hours. When I finally did look around I was going straight up to the landing-pier whence I had started.

"That is all of my story," he ended abruptly, starting to rise. "Keep it in your mind and plant it in your heart, and some day it may bear fruit in your life. How and when I know not, but this I know: What comes from God is eternal. What God has not planted will be rooted up; but what God has planted will bear fruit one hundred fold."

"Please wait a minute," I said. "What happened to you afterwards?"

"I merely took an elevator and went up to another floor. My life—the regular business and church life I had been living—went on as usual, but in an entirely different world. I found myself living thenceforth in a heavenly world where love and peace and happiness were everywhere about me in my life, with my business associates, and, yes, with the chance acquaintances I meet upon my travels." And he smiled at me.

"But how did you get up to that higher level?" I asked.

"It is a secret," he replied, "a great and wonderful secret. But if you really must know the secret, here it is: HE MAKETH MY FEET LIKE HIND'S FEET AND SETTETH ME UPON

MY HIGH PLACES.'' I started. ''Hind's feet!'' The words had been ringing in my ears for months. At last I had found the man—the man of mystery. At last I had caught up with the story that my friends had started to tell me.

''That is all.'' And again he started to rise.

''But can you explain what you mean by hind's feet?'' I begged.

''Does God explain to the deer how they are to use their feet?'' he asked enigmatically. ''No, they just use them. Go forth, son, and use them.''

''But may I ask one more question?'' I asked hesitatingly.

''Certainly.''

''What trail, what track do the hinds use when they go to the high places?''

He smiled. ''The best trail that I have found is the Lord's Prayer.'' And he rose, handed me his card, and went away.

I looked at the card, expecting to find some mysterious name fresh from fairyland. But there it stood, quite plain and prosaic—Mr. Fiebeger, of Akron, Ohio.

My journey was ended. I went to Grinnell and to Des Moines, and a few days later back to Grinnell, where I was married, and with my bride I returned to my college town.

In the meantime I almost forgot the old white-haired gentleman and his story. Indeed, I might have dismissed the entire episode as a dream and the man as a figment of my imagination, had it not been for one very tangible and startling incident that happened to me as soon as I reached the college town.

I took my wife into a rambling house which I had rented for our first home. I went down to fix the furnace, an immense soft-coal furnace with octopus arms holding up the house. I had thrown one shovelful of coal into its mouth and stood, poised, shovel in hand, ready to toss in the second, when I saw something that made my jaw drop and the coal spill to the floor. There above the door to the furnace was a name-plate bearing the inscription, The Fiebeger-Akron Furnace Company! So Mr. Fiebeger was a real man, after all! I had good reason to know, for the product of his factory warmed our home that first winter of our married lives! Yes, I have a still deeper reason to know, for the words of his heart have been warming my life ever since! If I needed anything more to convince me that he was not a dream, but a fact, it came a few months later when I received a copy of the Western *Christian Advocate* with a picture of "The Largest Men's Bible Class in the World, the First Methodist Church of Akron, Ohio, Mr. Fiebeger, Leader."

But dream or not, the seed he planted was not a dream, but was a reality. Nine years after this it suddenly opened its hard casing and started to bear fruit—fifty, sixty, and one hundred fold.

Nine years had gone by and I had forgotten about the old gentleman and his hind's feet, when circumstances led to my spending a few weeks on a Wyoming ranch. It was not a dude ranch, but the real thing. At my request a horse was turned over to me for my private use, and I was privileged to rough it with the cowboys in any manner I wished. I discovered that my horse was the fastest horse on the range. I wondered why this honor had been bestowed upon me. But I soon learned that while speed may be the most important thing on the plains, there is something much more significant on the mountains.

One day five of us were riding up the steep mountain-side to salt the cattle that roamed the plateau above. Everything went well until we came to a dangerous, slippery, craggy place, where a misstep would send us all to eternity. Then it was that the men advised me to take the less dangerous pathway that led by a slower route to the mountain top. When I asked them why I, alone, was asked to take this safer route, the foreman answered: "It is because your horse is not dependable on the hills. All the rest of our horses are true climbers—their rear feet track exactly where the forefeet are planted. When they place their forefoot upon a safe ridge, their rear foot will follow safely, too. But your horse, unfortunately, spent several years in the cities, and he lost the gift. Like all other animals over-exposed to modern civilization, his rear feet miss the front tracks by about two or three inches, and we are now going up trails where a miss of even an inch might mean death."

"I see," I replied. "Your horses have feet like the deer and the antelope."

"Exactly," he replied. "And a horse has to be as sure-footed as a mountain goat to take this trail to the high places."

And then a great light burst upon me. As I took that winding road that day I was glad to be alone, for the secret of the old white-haired gentleman was at last mine. The mystery of the hind's feet was solved. The deeper I got into the mystery the more marvelous it became. Thick and fast great thoughts came to me—thoughts that were as blinding as revelations. Here are a few of them, as best I can recall them:

No animal has such perfect correlation of its front and rear feet as does the deer. While the male deer, or the hart, is a wonder of surefootedness, still more wonderful is the female, or the hind, which, while leading its young into hidden fastnesses, is the most perfect example of physical correlation that God has ever made.

And this was the blinding revelation: *As the feet of the hind are to the mountains, so is the mind of man to the heights of life; and as the rear feet of the hind are to the front feet, so is the subconscious mind of man to the conscious mind.* And as the creature which has the most perfect correlation between its front and its rear feet is the surest to reach the mountain top in safety, so the person who has the most perfect correlation between his conscious mind and his subconscious mind is the surest to reach the heights of life.

"And he maketh my feet like hind's feet: and setteth me upon my high places." The Secret was revealed at last. I now knew what Jesus meant when He said, "Have faith in God. For verily I say unto you, that whosoever shall say unto this mountain, be thou removed and be thou cast into the sea; and shall not doubt *in his heart*, but shall believe that these things which he saith cometh to pass; he shall have whatsoever he saith. Yea, if ye have faith, though it be even as a grain of mustard seed, ye shall ask what ye will; and *nothing* shall be impossible unto you." Our lips speak the thoughts of our *conscious* mind, but only the *heart* speaks the thoughts of our subconscious mind. "As a man thinketh in his heart, so is he." "Out of the heart come the issues of life." And when the lips and the heart are in alignment, when they track together with the absolute certainty that the rear feet of the deer track with the front feet, then *nothing* is impossible, whether it be the climbing of mountains or the casting of mountains into the seas. The wonder of this burst upon me with such force that I could hardly wait until I could get back to my work and put my new discovery to the test.

I now saw that I had been missing the greatest blessings of life—and merely by inches. But in these seemingly trivial inches lay the secret of the supreme power and security of the seers and the saints and the prophets who lived in the mountains. By the mere fraction of an inch by which the rear feet of my city horse missed the security of the front feet, by merely that inch my life and the purposes of my life had been endangered. Only he who goes into the mountains in the morning and prays knows this secret. And so I, with the rest of the blind people of the cities and towns, had been taking the wide gate and the broad way that led to failure and futility, when all we needed to do was to change our feet to hind's feet and climb straight to the heights. "Enter ye in at the strait gate," came ringing into my ears as I rode along, "for wide is the gate, and broad is the way, that leadeth to destruction, and many there be which go in thereat. Because strait is the gate, and narrow is the way, which leadeth unto life, and few there be that find it." But he who has made his feet into hind's feet will find that climbing this narrow way is not so hard as many think.

"I have found the way! I have found the way!" my soul was singing. But I knew that I must not get excited. Much hard thinking and still harder work was to be done. Where did my conscious and subconscious mind track together? This was one of the first questions to be answered. How many things had I done with all my strength, with all my mind, and with all my heart, and with all my soul—in other words, with "all four feet"?

Pitifully few, I had to confess to myself. Had I spent so many years in the cities of materialism that my feet, like the feet of my horse, had lost their secret of correlation?

I had taught my students the little front-feet laws of writing, called grammar and rhetoric; how many had I taught the laws of the hind's feet and how to climb to the high places of true vision? I had filled hundreds of students' minds with knowledge; how many souls had I filled with faith? Many bachelors of arts had passed through my classes; how many prophets had I inspired? I could count those I had given passing grades by the hundreds; in how many had I awakened the hearts of poets? Many were the athletes I had coached; how many had I made into athletes of the spirit? I had been filling my mind with knowledge of things; did I know any more about the stars than my ancestors knew? I had accumulated a little house, a little insurance, a little nest egg toward my old age; how much wealth did I have that could be carried on my journey into the next stage of life? All around me was a multitude of things to take care of; how many things did I own? These were the questions that would not sleep, the doubts that would not stay outside my warmed and lighted room, and the more I postponed the answer to them the louder and more insistent they became, until they finally merged themselves into one great, insistent, clamoring question which would not be silenced, saying, "What shall it profit a man if he shall gain the whole world, and lose his own soul?"

From that day forth I let nothing stand between me and the making of my feet into hind's feet as fast as I could. And with each new victory new vistas, new visions opened upon my view. People began to come to me for help, for strength, for inspiration. But I was not satisfied in merely helping them; I wanted them to make their own feet into hind's feet so that they, too, could help others. For I have made this discovery that what every city needs, every community needs, every institution needs, every church needs, every neighborhood needs, more than it needs money or buildings or things, is a man or woman who can meet the description given in Isa. 32:2, "And a man shall be as a hiding-place from the wind, and a covert from the tempest; as streams of water in a dry place, as the shadow of a great rock in a weary land."

And that is why I have written this book, to help you be that man for your home, your community, your neighborhood.

INTERLUDE

Jesus likened the man who hears His words, and *does them*, unto a man who built his house upon a rock; and he who hears and does them not He likened unto a man who built his house upon sand. For too many years I have watched myself and other people build houses upon sand. I am not interested in sand houses any more. Unless you are ready to build upon rock there is nothing worth reading in this book. But if you would be a DOER, then follow directions just as definitely as an athlete would follow instructions of his coach. If you wish a seat in the grand stand you have entered this amphitheater by the wrong door. This book is a doorway straight to the field of action. Only athletes of the spirit are allowed to enter here.

Once a Persian philosopher came to a missionary and offered to pay him to read the Bible for an hour each day, and translate to him as he read. The offer was gladly accepted and the missionary read from the Bible for one hour. Finally he came to the passage, "Even so the tongue is a little member and boasteth great things—but the tongue can no man tame," at which the philosopher rose abruptly and said, "That will be enough for this day." He did not return for three months. The missionary expressed surprise that he had not returned sooner. "I thought you wanted me to read to you every day." "I did," replied the other, "but it took me this long to get that much."

I am going to ask you to turn to the following pages of this book with the same earnestness of spirit, and the same tenacity of purpose, as the Persian philosopher. Read one lesson at a time, and do not proceed to the next until you "get that much." Come to each day's reading like an athlete, stripped for action.

As you turn these pages you are not reading a book, but you are traveling up a mountain. You cannot read this book through at one sitting and get what it really contains. You will miss the greatest, the most precious, part of it, which is the "growing" part.

It took many years for the seeds planted by the old white-haired gentleman to incubate in my soul before they sprouted. After that there followed another period of time before I began to reap the harvest. Altogether in the planting and plowing and harvesting I have been traveling the path of the hind's feet over twenty-five years. I cannot hope to give you a quarter of a century of experience in one day. If you will give this study one hour a day of patient, honest, steady journeying, and if you will consent for one month to abide patiently by the directions which have been written down, in the spirit and under the guidance of prayer, some day you will reach the mountain top, and when you have reached the mountain top you will have found the greatest gift that God can give to man—the gift of God Himself.

This is to be a partnership affair. Lightning never strikes from above, but always from below. The first streak of lightning comes from the sky, it is true, but it is a very thin, weak streak, merely a "pathfinder." The technical name given to it by scientists is the "leader." Then up this path, marked by the "leader," the great voltage from the earth booms and crashes, and all that is achieved is achieved not by the "leader," but by that which comes from within the earth itself.

This book is merely a "leader." You yourself are to furnish the voltage if anything of great moment occurs within your own life. I have written the smaller half, you are to write the larger half. Before you start the next day's reading procure a notebook. In this notebook put from time to time, first, the exercises suggested by the various chapters; second, a prayer list of people for whom you want to pray; third, a prayer list of things for which you want to pray; fourth, poems and Bible quotations which help you to convert your feet into hind's feet.

How to Read This Book

First, devote a week to each chapter and the seven daily studies which follow it, before you turn to the next chapter; second, if you are one who must read a book right through in two or three sittings, read the five chapters and all of the Twelve Parable Miracles, but skip *all* of the daily studies, then return and spend a month taking each day's study in sequence, re-reading the chapters as you come to them.

FIRST DAY

HALLOWED BE THY NAME IN EARTH
AS IT IS IN HEAVEN

This winter my wife and I took a two weeks' trip through the South, and left our two daughters to look after the home while we were gone. To simplify the financial details I left a few checks definitely filled out for definite amounts, to such firms as the telephone company, where we knew exactly what the bill would be. But I also added a couple of "blank checks," properly signed, for the girls to use in case of emergency; to be properly filled out for whatever amount the emergency required.

Now I must state frankly that I should have been very much hurt, indeed, had my daughters taken those checks, the moment I got out of sight, and torn them up, saying to each other: "Our father is a good promiser, but he never makes good his promises. We are not going to cling to any old superstition that any sane storekeeper will honor these checks of our father's."

I admit that I am a college professor. I admit that there have been times when my deposit has been pretty low in the bank. I admit that these checks were written on "scraps of paper." But I know that my grocer, my baker, and all the other merchants with whom I do business have come to honor these "scraps of paper," not only with their conscious minds but with their subconscious minds. In fact, they accept them, literally as well as figuratively, "with all four feet." I was very happy when I returned from my trip to find that my daughters had trusted my name in my absence, as they trusted it when I was present.

Let us pause and think for one moment what miracles could happen in this world, if we should sincerely and earnestly HALLOW OUR FATHER'S NAME IN EARTH AS IT IS HALLOWED IN HEAVEN!

Our Father has left us promises written on what look like scraps of paper, promises which are meant to care for us until we can see Him some day, face to face. What if we should tear these up, saying: "Our Father is a good promiser, but He never makes good His promises. We are not going to cling to any old superstition that anyone on earth still believes in His promises." You know and I know that that is exactly what we do in actions, if not in words, time after time. If the subconscious mind of mankind should hallow, with the same surety and certainty, the name of God as we honor our great financiers—our Rockefellers, our Fords, and our Morgans—and if we trusted God's promises with the same surety and certainty that we respect the names and checks of men, there would be no dream impossible of fulfillment.

Now let me say, with all the faith and fervor of my being, that never were gilt-edged securities issued by any corporation in the United States, more sound and certain than the promises of God. The checks of men, above those needed for paying our daily bills, are usually placed in banks or invested in bonds and stocks that are subject to fluctuations of Wall Street. But no fluctuations have yet been able to deflate by one jot or tittle the value in the Great Promises stored away in the vaults of the Great Bank of God, "where neither moth nor rust doth corrupt, and where thieves do not break through nor steal."

Only one thing is required before we can convert the checks of God into the current specie of mankind and start them into circulation—and that is to hallow and respect the name of God who made the promises, not as His name is hallowed and respected in the conventional

Sabbath worship of earth, but *hallowed as it is in heaven*.

I admit that this is a tremendous requirement. It means that we must lift up our eyes unto the hills. It means that we must convert our feet into "hind's feet." Only one man in a thousand, or in ten thousand, seems capable of hallowing the name of God and respecting His power. George Müller did it. Wilfred Grenfell did it. Would you like to try it? Because there are so few is no reason why you cannot be one of them. Pray, first of all, for a faith that is equal to this great requirement, and then step up to the window of God's love and countersign His promises with a signature that says, "Father, I believe in Your Word."

If we human fathers are thoughtful in providing for our children, our Heavenly Father, whose heavenly love is infinitely greater than our human love, and whose heavenly foresight is infinitely more far-seeing than our human foresight, has left for us some definite promises concerning definite things, and then, in His infinite thoughtfulness, He has added a number of "blank checks" which we may use in cases of emergency for whatever we happen to need.

Here is an example of a definite promise to one asking guidance. "In all thy ways acknowledge Him, and He shall direct thy paths" (Prov. 3:6). Here is an example of a "blank check" which may be used for anything, "And whatsoever ye shall ask in My name, that will I do, that the Father may be glorified in the Son" (John 14:13).

Christ has left us ten blank checks, seven of which we may write in "whatsoever" we need. Could any gift be greater? But with great gifts go great responsibilities. When I left the blank checks with my daughters I knew that they would not write out a check for a thousand dollars and leave their college work and rush off for a wild trip through Europe; at least not until they had consulted me and received some definite guidance in the matter. In the same way our Heavenly Father trusts us to use, not only our common sense, but at least a fair amount of filial piety in consulting Him and awaiting His guidance, before we fill in His "blank checks" with unreasonable demands.

One of the remarkable privileges of these blank checks of God's is that we may use them over and over again with a new set of requests, and the more they are used, with faith, the more powerful they become. As that is the case, perhaps you will let me help you fill in these blank checks the first day. A safe rule for beginners in this "mountain-top banking" is to make your requests of the Father on as high a spiritual plane as possible.

Seven Whatsoever Checks on the Bank of God

(Sign your name on blank line and date check)

(1) Pay to the order of _____

I pray for Thy spirit to enter me and fill me completely.

"Therefore I say unto you what things soever ye desire, when ye pray, believe that ye receive them, and ye shall have them" (Mark 11:24).

In the name of Jesus Christ.

(2) Pay to the order of _____

I pray for Thy kingdom to come, in earth as it is in heaven.

"And whatsoever ye shall ask in My name, that will I do, that the Father may be glorified in the Son" (John 14:13).

In the name of Jesus Christ.

(3) Pay to the order of _____

I pray for my will to become completely and utterly Thy will.

"Verily, verily I say unto you, Whatsoever ye shall ask the Father in My name, He will give it to you" (John 16:23).

In the name of Jesus Christ.

(4) Pay to the order of _____

I pray for my actual needs to be met by the right supply, in the right way and at the right time.

"And whatsoever we ask, we receive of Him, because we keep His commandments, and do those things that are pleasing in His sight" (1 John 3:22).

In the name of Jesus Christ.

(5) Pay to the order of _____

I pray for the right persons to come into my life, at the right time and in the right way.

"And if we know that He hear us, whatsoever we ask, we know that we have the petitions that we desired of Him" (1 John 5:15).

(6) Pay to the order of _____

I pray for the right ideas to come to me in perfect sequence and in perfect order, in the right time and in the right way.

In the name of Jesus Christ.

"Ye have not chosen me, but I have chosen you . . . that ye should go and bring forth fruit, and that your fruit should remain; that whatsoever ye shall ask of the Father in My name, He may give it to you" (John 15:16).

In the name of Jesus Christ.

(7) Pay to the order of _____

I pray for my deepest soul's sincere desire to be fulfilled in the right time and in the right way.

"But I know, that even now, whatsoever thou wilt ask of God, God will give it thee" (John 11:22).

In the name of Jesus Christ.

Now look over this list. If these things were granted you, there would be a real heaven on earth for you. Are you asking too much? Don't be afraid to aim high! Remember that every promise of God is backed by the golden reserves of the Great Bank of Heaven. Just take those seven checks to the Bank of God tonight in prayer, and ask Him to redeem them for you, in His own way and in His own time.

MEDITATION

As the rain cometh down, and the snow from heaven, and returneth not thither, but watereth the earth, and maketh it to bring forth and bud, that it may give seed to the sower, and bread to the eater: so shall My word be that goeth forth out of My mouth: it shall not return unto Me void, but it shall accomplish that which I please, and it shall prosper in the thing whereto I sent it (Isa. 55:10-11). (Read Ps. 8.)

PRAYER

Our Father Who art in Heaven, forgive us for our failure to honor Thee as we should, in the past. Help us to hallow Thy Name, and honor Thy Message, and trust Thy Word even as the dewdrop trusts itself to the sun, and the river gives itself to the sea. Amen.

SECOND DAY

THY KINGDOM COME IN EARTH AS IT IS IN HEAVEN

The second "Whatsoever promise" you cashed in on yesterday was "Thy Kingdom Come, in earth as it is in heaven." What we asked for yesterday, as through a glass darkly, today we are now going to try to see face to face.

What is the Kingdom of Heaven? Our first thought, naturally, is of a gloriously blissful place "over there," a place which we shall have to wait to experience, after our death. But the Lord's Prayer of Jesus makes the very definite request for this Kingdom to come into manifestation within our lives here and *now*, while living on this earth.

An answer to this prayer, for heaven to be manifest upon earth, would naturally be a blissful, harmonious relationship between all persons, where each one leads a perfectly adjusted and harmonious life, in perfectly adjusted and harmonious relationship with all other lives—climaxed and crowned by a perfect relationship, through love and adoration, with the Heavenly Father.

The place for this Kingdom to begin is right within your own self. Jesus made it very clear that we need waste no time trying to set up an external Kingdom, until we have first found the roots and foundation of it within. Our first great discovery is that each one of us is a focalized expression, as it were, of all of the infinite harmonies of heaven. The best description of this, as a positive experience, has been written by Margaret Prescott Montague in "Twenty Minutes of Reality" which appeared in the *Atlantic Monthly*, November, 1916:

I was lying on a cot on the porch of a hospital at the time, convalescing after a serious illness. It was an ordinary cloudy March day. I am glad to think that it was. I am glad to remember that there was nothing extraordinary about the weather, nor any unusualness of setting—no flush of spring or beauty of scenery—to induce what I saw. It was, on the contrary, almost a dingy day.

Yet here, in this everyday setting, and entirely unexpectedly (for I had never dreamed of such a thing), my eyes were opened, and for the first time in all my life I caught a glimpse of the ecstatic beauty of reality. I cannot now recall whether the revelation came suddenly or gradually; I only remember finding myself in the very midst of those wonderful moments, beholding life for the first time in all its young intoxication of loveliness, in its unspeakable joy, beauty, and importance. I cannot say exactly what the mysterious change was. I saw no new thing, but I saw all the usual things in a miraculous new light—in what I believe is their true light. I saw for the first time how wildly beautiful and joyous, beyond any words of mine to describe, is the whole of life. Every human being moving across that porch, every sparrow that flew, every branch tossing in the wind, was caught in and was a part of the whole mad ecstasy of loveliness, of joy, of importance, of intoxication of life.

It was not that for a few keyed-up moments I IMAGINED all existence so beautiful, but that my inner vision was cleared to the truth so that I SAW the actual loveliness which is always there, but which we so rarely perceive; and I knew that every man, woman, bird, and tree, every living thing before me, was extravagantly beautiful and extravagantly important. And as I beheld, my heart melted out of me in a rapture of love and delight.

For those glorified moments I was in love with every living thing before me—the trees in the wind, the little birds flying, the nurses, the internes, the people who came and went. There was nothing that was alive that was not a miracle. Just to be alive was a miracle in itself. My very soul flowed out of me in a great joy.

For those fleeting lovely moments I did in deed and in truth love my neighbor as myself. Nay more: of myself I was hardly conscious, while with my neighbor in every form, from wind-tossed branches and little sparrows flying, up to human beings, I was madly in love.

This is how, for me, all fear of eternity has been wiped away. I have found a little taste of bliss, and if Heaven can offer this, no eternity will be too long to enjoy the miracle of existence. But that was not the greatest thing that those twenty minutes revealed, and that did most to end all fear of life everlasting. The great thing was the realization that weariness, and boredom, and questions as to the use of it all, belong entirely to unreality. When once we wake to Reality—whether we do so here or have to wait for the next life for it—we shall never be bored, for in Reality there is no such thing.

Milton says:

What if earth be but the shadow of Heaven,
and things therein each to the other like,
more than on earth is thought.

What if here we are only symbols of ourselves, and our real being is somewhere else—perhaps in the heart of God?

You, too, have had authentic experiences of the reality of the Kingdom. Have you ever had an experience, at any time, of actual living, even for a moment in the Kingdom of Heaven, where the inner happiness and harmony were so real, that they simply *had* to manifest in outer love and harmony? Did you ever find yourself with the person you wanted to be with when you wanted to be with him, and find that at the same time he wanted to be with you? If you did you have experienced one of the very real and authentic foretastes of heaven. Have you ever, either when making a speech or conversing with a friend, found your ideas coming in perfect sequence and in perfect order, just the right ideas at the right time and in the right way? If you did you have experienced another very authentic foretaste of heaven. Now turn back to the several "Whatsoever prayers" as listed on pages 18-20. If these were all answered eternally and continually, including the one you added as your deepest soul's sincere desire, you would not only be actually living in heaven, but you would be creating a heavenly atmosphere all around you, for others to live in as well."

"The Kingdom of God is within you," says Jesus, which means to say that it is a state of consciousness. But it is a creative (not a stagnant) state of consciousness, which, once realized within, gradually manifests itself outwardly in those things which are capable of making the inner state of harmony permanent. The Kingdom of Heaven, in other words, is that state of peace which is so dynamic and creative that it can no more be kept invisible than steam can be kept in a teakettle.

The Kingdom of Heaven begins as something too infinitesimally small to be seen by the naked eye. But it does not remain small and invisible any more than a seed once planted in the ground remains invisible. I am reiterating that because it is important that you remember it. This creative consciousness steadily grows and unfolds ntil it becomes a many-branched tree, and the birds of heaven come and lodge in its branches.

Glance back at the seven "Whatsoever" requests on pages 23-25 and see how the fulfillment of these requests would contribute greatly toward bringing this Kingdom of Heaven into your life. Fortunately, Jesus did not give us only these seven "Whatsoever" blank checks, he also gave us three "Anything" blank checks. Let us use these three now to ask the Father for the beautiful state of consciousness which brought Margaret Montague her marvelous experience.

(1) *Grant to me, O Father, the power to love everybody and everything.*

"If ye shall ask *any thing* in My name, I will do it" (John 14:14).

(2) *Grant to me, O Father, the capacity to see everything as intensely and ecstatically beautiful.*

"Again I say unto you, that if two of you shall agree on earth as touching *any thing* that they shall ask, it shall be

(3)   *Grant to me, O Father, the ability to see infinite value and importance in everything that God has made.*

done for them of My Father which is in heaven" (Matt. 18:19).

"And this is the confidence that we have in Him, that, if we ask *any thing* according to His will He heareth us" (I John 5:14).

MEDITATION

And I saw a new heaven and a new earth; for the first heaven and the first earth were passed away; and there was no more sea. And I, John, saw the holy city, new Jerusalem, coming down from God out of heaven, prepared as a bride adorned for her husband. And I heard a great voice out of heaven saying, Behold, the tabernacle of God is with men, and He will dwell with them, and they shall be His people, and God Himself shall be with them, and be their God. Revelation 21:1-3. (Read Matt. 25:14-30.)

PRAYER

Our heavenly Father, make us unresisting instruments for helping to bring Thy Kingdom of Heaven, in all its love and beauty and harmony, from invisibility into visibility, into the hearts of men.

THIRD DAY

THY WILL BE DONE IN EARTH AS IT IS IN HEAVEN

"The Kingdom," says Henry Nelson Weiman, "was Jesus' word for the total maximum of possibility for good which can be accomplished in us, and through us, and around about us, inasmuch as we make right adaptation to God."

How can we make right adaptation to God? The simplest way of answering this is in the statement, Making our will God's will.

For the past two days we have made requests of God, as though He were to do all of the answering. That is only half. We can help to answer our own prayers. This answering of prayers is a partnership affair. With each request goes a corollary: We must be willing to meet God halfway. For instance, in asking God to send us the right people at the right time, we must be willing to accept those people He does send to us, even though at first glance, they may not seem to be exactly the ones whom we should have chosen. We must keep open minds and open hearts, and make an honest effort to *want* to be with them. We shall then find that part of this new magic is the transformation that goes on within ourselves. As old prejudices and old enmities in our hearts vanish away, we shall see old enemies and unwelcome neighbors transforming themselves into loving and welcome friends.

We must also be patient with the seemingly poor ideas, and stupid lapses and bungling mistakes we ourselves sometimes make when trusting to God. In other words, as we grow more forgiving and tolerant of others, we must also forgive our own past errors as well. We must accept the fact that God had some good reason—perhaps to humble us—in letting us make an apparent blunder or stupid mistake. "Forgetting that which is behind," as Paul puts it, let us keep on trusting God in our period of apprenticeship, doing the best we can, being willing to "go halfway," and we shall find that this period of apprenticeship and discipline will be shortened. Our mistakes will grow less. God's discipline will grow less. And the manifestation of heaven in our life can be a more immediate thing than we ever imagined it could be. Let us not grow impatient with God's discipline.

Before a football-player makes the team, the coach often tries him out for a season on the scrubs. Before you meet the glorious ones God is planning for you to meet, He may want you to help some weary and stupid ones whom you will not have the opportunity to meet in the future, or, He may want you to forgive your enemies of yesterday before He opens the door for the new and glorious friends of tomorrow. Indeed, I have found it a common practice of many booklovers never to open a new chapter until the old chapter is completed. God has a way of working like that. Whenever He does a thing He does it completely. He never leaves a thing half done. So, if there are any old enemies you have not forgiven in the past, do not delay in wiping the slate clean, in order to speed up your meeting with the wonderful new friends waiting for you out there in the future. Let me repeat, the first lesson God gives us in training our will is in making us go halfway with Him. He first puts us through a series of disciplines to see if we are worthy to make His team. After this lesson is learned we discover that there are many, many times that God goes *all* the way with *us*. Over and over again He gives us far more than we have any right to ask. We call this "His Grace," which goes so much farther than "His Law" requires that He should go. God's mercy goes so much farther than mere human justice goes.

And then there are many times when God gives us the opportunity to go *all* the way with Him. He did that with Job. He did it with Abraham. He used it as a school for

many of His greatest saints and leaders. One of the great
privileges He may give to you—if He is preparing you for
great leadership—is the opportunity sometime of going
all the way with Him. One of those who did this was
Thomas à Kempis. Hear his profession of faith:

> O Lord, Thou knowest what is the better way; let this or
> that be done as Thou shalt please. Give what Thou wilt, and
> how much Thou wilt, and when Thou wilt. Deal with me as
> Thou knowest, and best pleaseth Thee, and is most for Thy
> honor. Set me where Thou wilt, and deal with me in all things
> as Thou wilt. I am in Thy hand; turn me round and turn me
> back again, even as a wheel. Behold I am Thy servant, pre-
> pared for all things; for I desire not to live unto myself, but
> unto Thee; and Oh that I could do it worthy and perfectly!

To make God's will your will is to go all the way with
God. This requires more complete, utter surrender of self
than anything you have ever done before. It means making God the senior partner in your firm, and trusting
completely in Him. Then all that you need to do is to see
that your *intention* is right. God will look after the *result*.

The first two days you have written down the things
you wanted. Some attention was naturally focused on
the results you would like to have come to pass. Today I
am going to ask you to try to give no heed to results.
Make no personal requests of your own, whatsoever. Let
your prayer be that all results may be God's results. "Thy
will, not mine be done." That means that all RESULTS
THAT GOD SEES FIT TO BRING TO PASS WILL BE SATISFACTORY
TO YOU.

Not only does making your will God's will bring you
peace, but it also brings you perfect understanding. "IF

ANY MAN WILL DO HIS WILL HE SHALL KNOW OF THE DOC-
TRINE" (John 7:17). But more is required than just to *know*.
You must *experience* this surrender to the will of God.

Repeat aloud twenty times, as though each statement
were carrying you up the last step to the "high places" of
God, this assertion: I *will* to *will* the WILL of God. Repeat
it until the subconscious mind vibrates with the conscious mind. This resolution, when made with a clear realization, will prove sufficient, if your feet are hind's feet,
to set you on high places. When this surrender of your
will completely to the Father's will begins to be a living
realization in the deepest areas of your being, then you
will have learned the third lesson of making your feet
"hind's feet."

In the sentence given above there are three *wills*. The
first is the man will, the third is the God will, the second
is the will-in-action. Once bring the first and last wills
into perfect alignment and they will bring to birth that
will which manifests itself in action. When God's larger
will completely eclipses your smaller will, a marvelous
thing immediately happens in your life. From that moment you rejoice and take delight in anything that
furthers the Great Plan of God—for henceforth God's
plan is your plan, and your plan is God's plan. All responsibility drops from your shoulders; all results are
God's results. Merely start out each day as God's man,
and let Him direct every step of the way.

For today exercise this surrender of the will by memo-
rizing both the Meditation and the Prayer that follow, and
repeating them to yourself many times during the week.

MEDITATION
Commit thy way unto the Lord; trust also in Him, and

He shall bring it to pass (Ps. 37:5). In all thy ways acknowledge Him, and He shall direct thy paths (Prov. 3:6). (Read Ps. 18:1, 2, 30–36.)

PRAYER

(from St. Ignatius Loyola.)

Take, O Lord, and receive my entire liberty, my memory, my understanding, and my whole will. All that I am, all that I have, Thou hast given me, and I will give it back again to Thee to be disposed of according to Thy good pleasure. Give me only Thy love and Thy grace; with Thee I am rich enough, nor do I ask for aught besides.

FOURTH DAY

GIVE US THIS DAY OUR DAILY BREAD

We prayed on the first day that our hearts should be God's, on the second day that our minds should be God's, and on the third day that our wills should be God's. Today let us pray that our bodies shall be God's. Good people, who think that they have a right to pray for their souls, but not for their bodies, forget that two-thirds of Jesus' active ministry upon earth was concerned with the healing of human bodies. If we take Jesus as our model in all things, why should we hesitate to take Him as a model in this? I must confess that it took me years to overcome my prejudice against using prayer for the service of my body. The field of health and finance seemed to fall outside the realm of religion. I had forgotten that there is not a sparrow that falleth without the Father—that there is not a single area of our human life that falls outside the Father's loving jurisdiction.

This was borne in on me one day when a friend gave me some orange juice with many ice cubes in it. Ice cubes, made of water, tend to dilute the fruit juice and make it insipid. But, to my amazement, instead of reducing the flavor, the ice cubes positively improved it.

"You see," explained my hostess, "these ice cubes are frozen orange juice, so the more you use, the richer the drink."

This is the way we should think of our bodies. They are no more foreign to the spirit, than the ice cubes were foreign to the orange juice. They are merely solidified manifestations of the same thing. Strange how most of us think of our bodies as something apart from spirit, so far apart, indeed, that they not only *di*lute the spirit, but sometimes actually *pol*lute it.

How often we listen to a message of golden truth, every word of which we believe, but which has become vapid and insipid by the time it reaches our ears, because it has been so diluted by the covetous, conceited, selfish personality of the man who uttered it! It is the secret of Kagawa's message that the very *body* of his economic and his business life, and his home life, are all surrendered utterly to the Father. Like Jesus' garment, which was all of one piece and woven from above, so all of Kagawa's life is of God. It matters little whether it is in the fluid form of messages and sermons, or in the solid form of the body in which he is living—it is all of the same pattern, and all woven from God Himself.

The nectar of heaven is in the drink; it is also in the ice cubes. If this is so, when I ask my Father to fill me with His spirit in the form of ideas, emotions, and loves, why cannot I also ask Him to supply me with His substance in the form of houses and lands and money—yes, and healthy body as well? The little bee that made the honey also made the honeycomb to hold the honey; and the

Great God who made our souls made our bodies to hold our souls, and furnishes the bread to keep those bodies alive.

When Jesus gave His disciples wine and bread, the wine represented the inner, invisible elements of the invisible spirit; the bread represented the outer expression in form and substance and body. He told us that henceforth we were to be His spirits, carrying His Spirit to all men. And at the same time, He told us that we are to be His bodies, embodying His Word in our life and action in such a way as to bless all mankind. Paul tells us, "Now ye are the body of Christ" (I Cor. 12:27). Sweet is the *spirit* and also the *body* that carries the spirit, yes, sweet as the honey and the honeycomb are the spirit and the outer manifestation of the spirit in the bodies of men. The Holy Ghost and the Holy Spirit were almost interchangeable words in Jesus' vocabulary; therefore, if we can pray with faith, when we ask for an inspiration for our spirit, why can we not also pray with faith when we ask for bread for our bodies? These are the arguments I had to use for myself before I could bring my stubborn subconscious mind to accept the fact that there is nothing unheavenly or unspiritual in God's Kingdom, even our food and money— if we are utterly surrendered with "all four feet"—that is to say, with all our soul, and with all our mind, and with all our heart, and with all our strength—to the Lord our God.

Look over the seven "Whatsoever" requests you prayed for on pages 23-25 in the first day's meditation, and the three "Anything" requests you prayed for on pages 30-31 and let us add to these, three more magnificent promises of Jesus, and use them in asking for our "daily bread."

(1)   *I ask Thee, O Father, for the health and strength that will enable me to serve Thee, and never fail Thee.*

"Ask and it shall be given you . . . for everyone that asketh receiveth" (Mat. 7:7-8).

(2)   *I seek, from Thee, O Father, the money and things that will supply the resources for a creative and fruitful life.*

"Seek, and ye shall find . . . for he that seeketh findeth" (Matt. 7:7-8).

(3)   *Open the door, O Father, to the right work that will enable me to make my finest contribution to mankind.*

"Knock, and it shall be opened unto you . . . for to him that knocketh it shall be opened" (Matt. 7:7-8).

MEDITATION

Know ye not that ye are the temple of God, and that the Spirit of God dwelleth in you? (I Cor. 3:16). (Read Ps. 139:14-18, 23-24.)

PRAYER

Our Father, we know that Thou art the Bread of Life, he that cometh to Thee shall never hunger; Thou art the Water of Life, he that believeth on Thee shall never thirst. Make us pure channels for manifesting Thy love and Thy abundance in the daily round of life. Amen.

FIFTH DAY
FORGIVE US OUR TRESPASSES AS WE FORGIVE THOSE WHO TRESPASS AGAINST US

After these four days of "tuning in" with the Father, if your partnership with Him is not a "going concern," if you do not experience the lightness and love and joy that one should experience when his will is completely surrendered to the Father's will—if, in short, your feet are not entirely "hind's feet," then ask yourself honestly whether there is not some point where you are not "playing the game," where you are not holding up your part of the partnership as you should.

If you are completely and utterly God's, your mind and will and body utterly His, then today's meditation is not of much importance to you. But if you are not completely surrendered, then it holds the very key to your personal life and you are invited to spend hours, if necessary, to get the perfect cleansing and clearing that you need.

Read this next sentence very carefully, for in it lies the secret of the failure of half of the so-called Christians of the world to walk with "hind's feet" to the high places God has prepared for them. IF YOU HATE JUST ONE INDIVIDUAL IN THE WORLD, BY JUST THAT MUCH YOU ARE SEPARATED FROM GOD HIMSELF. By just that much do your rear feet fail to track with your front feet, and in the crises of life you are in danger of slipping over the ledge to failure. If God is ALL, then He manifests through *every* individual soul, and if every person is an individual child of God Himself, anything that separates you from one of God's children separates you from the Father.

If you have done any injustice to anyone, you have done an injustice to God. If you have hurt any human soul, you have hurt the Father Himself. If you have robbed, beaten, or slandered anyone, you have despitefully used the Father. If anyone has sinned against you and you have not forgiven him, you are hating and despising God. "If a man say I love God, and hateth his brother, he is a liar; for he that loveth not his brother whom he hath seen, how can he love God whom he hath not seen?'' Your first duty is to forgive others. Turn to all those who have trespassed against you and forgive them. Write down all the injustices that you can recall, that others have committed against *you*. There is a real purpose in this, for, if you remember a slight, nine times out of ten it is because you have not forgiven it. So, first of all, take up these sins that others have committed against you, and forgive them one by one. Forgive them completely and utterly. As a little sacrament to seal this forgiveness and make it final, put the list in the fireplace; light a match to it and let it go up in smoke, never to return again.

Now turn to one of the promises of Christ, not a blank check, this time, but a clear-cut promise of a very definite thing: "For if ye forgive men their trespasses, *your Heavenly Father will also forgive you*.'' Remember that this is just as "cashable'' a promise as any check that any millionaire ever wrote. Believe in it with all of your conscious and subconscious mind. Step out upon it with "all four feet.'' That minute you will be liberated from something that may have been blocking the free flow of God's blessings to you for years and years. Now you are ready to ask forgiveness for your own sins. Having forgiven those who have trespassed against *you*, ask God to forgive you for your trespasses against *others*.

Take a loose leaf of paper—do not write these sins in your notebook which is to be reserved for the permanent and *real* things—and write down these sins. Try to make the list as complete as you know how to make it. You are alone with God. No person is in the room with you. Only this open book is before you, listening as you speak out your own secret faults, and witnessing you as you write them down. And books carry no tales. Therefore you have the opportunity, if you will only use it, of indulging in an unusual luxury—*you can be honest, absolutely honest, with yourself.*

When your list is complete, look it over carefully.

Then look through each fault to the good thing of which it is the opposite, the shadow, or the counterfeit. For instance, behind the sin of greed lies the virtue of thrift, behind pride lies magnanimity, behind cruelty lies energy, behind lust lies love. Gambling is merely courage gone to seed, and drunkenness is the effort of a man to lose himself in a power greater than himself—his only trouble is that he is letting himself be led captive to the devil instead of to the Living God. Copy these virtues in your permanent notebook. Then take the loose sheet of paper on which you have written your temptations and your sins, and cast it into the fireplace and apply a match to it, and watch it go up in flames. As the dross of your life burns away, turn to the notebook filled now only with virtues, and see the clear molten gold that remains. Look at yourself as the son of God, cleansed of all of these things that have been dragging you down. Ask God to clothe you in the perfection that lies behind the seeming imperfection that has beset you and make you a perfect being in a perfect world, governed by a perfect God. Here, before the ashes of your old dead self, highly resolve to seek with all of the zeal and perseverance of the old gold seekers of '49, for the true courage, the true goodness, and the true inspiration of that *brand-new self which you so eagerly wish to become.*

But supposing there is one of these sins that is not disposed of so easily. Supposing, like the proverbial dandelion, that it has roots that do not come up when the rest of your sins are pulled up and cast into the fire. Supposing there is some old root—greed, lust, jealousy, or hate—that seems so ingrained in your very bones, in your very nervous system, in your very blood, that there is no way of getting it out. Then, lean back and let the Christ work the miracle.

When you recover from an illness is it because *you* do anything? No. All you do is to lie on the bed and rest, and the cleansing blood, continuously flowing through your veins, brings the healing. Kagawa says:

Blood has a strange power. First it cleanses the body of impurities, draws away the pus from injured tissues and restores them. Second, it even has the power of rebuilding tissues that have been destroyed. It builds not only skin and flesh, but, as in the case of the finger nail, it has the mysterious power of reproducing the structure and form as well. Third, the blood has the power of controlling the development of any part of the body, a power that reaches into the future.

The power of blood means the power of love! If blood can bring recovery to the sores of the body, love has the power to redeem the wounds of the personality. If blood has the power to restore broken-down tissues, love can make the wounded personality whole again, until it becomes a child of God. It is the teaching of the New Testament that the sacrificial love of Christ has this power to redeem, and make restitution for all the past sins of humankind. Not that physical blood can redeem the sins of the soul; but to love other men enough to be willing to pour out your blood for them, this is the acme of spiritual love. Such love has the power to redeem and in this lies the hidden reason why Christ poured out His blood upon the cross.[1]

[1]Kagawa in "Meditations on the Cross."

The world has seen much shedding of blood, blood shed for private advantage, or to satisfy selfish desires. But the blood which Christ shed was to save mankind, to redeem sinners, and to make the human race into children of God. We cannot doubt that the blood of the Cross is the purest and most precious blood shed in all history.[2]

Open your heart in absolute trust while this "purest and most precious blood in all history" brings you complete cleansing and healing. Open your soul while the love of Christ—"the acme of all spiritual love"—the love which has the power to save, and redeem the most hopeless of sinners—takes complete dominion over every area of your life. "Greater love hath no man than this, that a man lay down his life for his friends."

MEDITATION

Though your sins be as scarlet, they shall be as white as snow; though they be red like crimson, they shall be as wool (Isa. 1:18). As far as the east is from the west, so far hath He removed our transgressions from us (Ps. 103:12). For Thou, Lord, art good, and ready to forgive; and plenteous in mercy unto all them that call upon Thee (Ps. 86:5). (Read Ps. 32.)

PRAYER

Our Heavenly Father, we thank Thee that Thou art a God of unlimited compassion, willing and able to grant far more than we ask of Thee. Blot out all our transgressions, cleanse us of all iniquity, redeem our hungry, thirsting souls. Hold us fast in Thy love forever. Amen.

[2]Kagawa in "The Religious Herald."

SIXTH DAY
LEAD US NOT INTO TEMPTATION
BUT DELIVER US FROM EVIL

After one has pulled out from his deep subconscious the sins both of commission and omission, and forgiven and asked forgiveness for them, confessed and made restitution for them, he has gone far toward making himself immune from committing sins in the future. But there is something more to be done. Yesterday we considered *sins* of the *past*; today we consider *temptations* of the *future*. Yesterday you looked at the sins, listed them, burned them up. Today do not look at the evils, but at the good. Let us not look at the negatives that lead us into temptation, but let us look at the positives that lead us away from evil.

Let me tell you why I asked you to make a list of your sins yesterday, and, having looked them squarely in the face, burn them up. An act sometimes does something that mere thinking and wishing cannot do. Thinking plus acting—a thorough writing down and a thorough burning up—furnished an opportunity for you to bring all "four feet" into operation in the getting rid of sin. If you were able to do this with the "hind's feet" of humility, sincerity, earnestness, and faith, you may not need to dwell long on the meditation I have prepared for this day. But unless you got clear down to the deepest roots of sin in your deep subconscious self, there remains a little more to be done to protect you from temptation in the future.

Most of the things we have done in the past have set up some sort of record in the subconscious. How simple it would be if these were "phonograph records," and all we needed to do would be to pick them up and toss them out of the window. As a matter of fact it is as simple a matter as that when your faith is sincere, pure, and positive. But I want to tell you at this point that the subconscious (which stands as a watch-dog over these records) is sometimes very stubborn. It is very much indeed like an untamed beast. People who have had experience with dangerous animals know that an animal senses unerringly when you are trusting it, whether you are really friendly or whether you are pretending. If you are pretending, it at once gets excited and dangerous and you are in grave risk. The faith that will shut the mouths of lions must be more than a pious hope that they will not bite; it must be the creative faith that imposes its goodwill on the nervous, suspicious nature of the animal. The man who has conquered his own fear can conquer the beast. In the same way the subconscious mind is very shrewd, it knows when one is in earnest; no one ever has or ever will fool it by hypocrisy or pretense.

The Bible has given us several ways of convincing this subconscious mind that we mean what we say. The first is to look at the positives, not the negatives. "Rejoice not that the spirits are subject unto you; but rather rejoice, because your names are written in heaven." Look steadily at the good, not at the bad, at the things you want, not at the things of which you want to get rid. Do not look at Sodom, open your window toward Jerusalem, for "the land thou seest, to thee I will give it." Peter, walking on the water, was safe when he looked steadfastly at Jesus; he was in peril the moment he looked down at the sea. And yet there are many times when we must look at the bad, when we must open the wound and look at the poison, but only long enough to cleanse it. A brief look at the bad, and a long, persistent, determined look at the good—that is a good formula for convincing the subconscious that you are in earnest.

The second way of convincing the subconscious is persistence. By pure reiteration of the statement, "I will to will the will of God," or by repeating over and over and over again one of the promises—one of the signed checks of God—you may actually make the subconscious *believe* that you *mean* what you say.

Another way to convince the old watch-dog of your subconscious mind of your sincerity, is to resort to some symbolical or sacramental gesture that is so tied up with racial roots of the past that it creates absolute conviction upon the inner mind. The listing of your sins and the burning of them was such a sacrament, and a very real and vital one at that. The cleansing power of the blood of Jesus is one of the most sound sacraments in the history of religion. We do not need to use persistence, or symbology, or sacrament *to persuade God.* GOD IS PERFECTLY CAPABLE OF CLEANSING US INSTANTLY AND MAKING US IMPERVIOUS TO EVIL OF ANY KIND. HE IS ETERNALLY STANDING AT THE DOOR OF OUR CONSCIOUS SELF, WAITING EVERY MINUTE TO ENTER AND HEAL OUR SOULS, even as our own blood is ever ready to heal our bodies if we give it half a chance. We need these things to persuade, *not God, but our own stubborn subconscious self*. This is the doubting Thomas who stands as the porter at the door of our inner consciousness—barring God out, until we have persuaded it that we mean exactly what we say.

One cannot make a blood transfusion if the veins of the one to receive it are closed. Neither can the redeeming power of the blood of Christ wash our sins away unless the doors of our soul are opened through Repentance, Humility and Faith. Such Repentance and

Humility and Faith are best revealed when one shares his problems frankly with another soul. If everything else fails, we can go to the most surrendered and most understanding person we know, one who has the positive faith we crave, and completely surrender ourself in his presence, and ask him to help us give ourself over to the healing power of God.

Having done this with another we need not repeat it with him, and under no circumstances with anyone else. Our purpose has been to erase self, not to exhibit self. When one is once given into the hands of the Father, he is completely given. We should give ourselves so utterly to the task of filling ourselves with the Living Christ that there will be no room henceforth for that which is unlike Christ ever to enter again.

And to make this final, to help keep ourselves impervious against attacks of evil in the future, we should put on the whole armor of God. "Finally, my brethren, be strong in the Lord, and in the power of His might. Put on the whole armor of God, that ye may be able to stand against the wiles of the devil. For we wrestle not against flesh and blood, but against principalities, against powers, against the rulers of the darkness of this world, against spiritual wickedness in high places. Wherefore take unto you the whole armor of God, that ye may be able to withstand in the evil day, and having done all to stand. Stand, therefore, having your loins girt about with *truth*, and having on the breastplate of *righteousness*; and your feet shod with the preparation of the gospel of *peace*; above all, taking the shield of *faith*, wherewith ye shall be able to quench all the fiery darts of the wicked. And take the helmet of *salvation*, and the sword of the *Spirit*, which is the Word of God. Praying always with all prayer and supplication in the Spirit" (Eph. 6:10-18).

One cannot find any better armor to protect oneself against recurring attacks of temptation than this armor of God. Clothed in TRUTH and RIGHTEOUSNESS, very little can penetrate us. Shod with sandals of PEACE, no stone or rocky path can hurt our feet and endanger our journey.

The helmet of SALVATION is the very grace of God Himself surrounding our thoughts, our subconscious as well as our conscious thoughts, holding our hearts and our minds in Christ Jesus, so that nothing can hurt us. The shield of FAITH upon our left arm can then quench *all* the burning darts of the evil one, and hold us impervious to all evil. The sword of the SPIRIT, which is the word of God—the irresistible promises of God—will enable us to grow in grace and strength and the power to help and protect others. Just to vision ourselves so clad and so protected is to hold ourselves in a state of continuous prayer, "Praying always with all prayer and supplication, in the Spirit."

MEDITATION

Be strong and of a good courage, fear not, nor be afraid of them; for the Lord thy God, He it is that doth go with thee; He will not fail thee, nor forsake thee (Deut. 31:6). (Read Ps. 121.)

PRAYER

Our Heavenly Father, henceforth we shall have no fear, for we trust utterly in Thee, and Thou art the God of Love, Giver of every good and perfect gift. Resting in Thee, and abiding eternally in Thy love, we are impervious as in a cita-

del, for no evil can henceforth reach us without first passing through Thee, being transformed in the process into perfect purity, perfect harmony, and perfect love. Hold us close to Thy Heart, O Father, and accept our gratitude, our adoration, and our love. Amen.

SEVENTH DAY

FOR THINE IS THE KINGDOM AND THE POWER AND THE GLORY FOR EVER

And now that the house is cleaned, throw wide open the doors and let the Christ enter in. This is much easier than you think, that is if you have made a pretty thorough job of emptying out your little selfish self, *and if you have a truly great desire that He come in*. For as nature cannot permit a vacuum, neither can God permit a vacuum. As all the seven seas are stirred to fill the little well that the child has dug in the seashore sand, so all heaven is stirred from its heights to its depths to fill the heart that truly hungers after God. Christ, whose great heart seeks and hungers for us, even more than our hearts hunger for Him, permits neither principalities nor powers, nor things present nor things to come, nor height nor depth, nor any other creature, to separate us from the most tender, the most virile, the most irresistible expression of the love of God, that man has ever known.

And when this beautiful expression of the incarnate love of God enters us, Christ is no longer an external Saviour. He is henceforth within us. Just as the electric-light power is actually and literally in the light bulb, so Christ is actually and literally within you. He thereafter constitutes Himself your very life, taking you into union with Himself, your body, mind, and spirit. While you still have your own identity and free will and moral responsibility, henceforth you need never ask Him again to help you, as though He were one and you another. Henceforth you need simply do your duty, and know you are doing His duty, you need act only upon your own surrendered and guided will, and you are doing His will. Your body is His body, your mind is His mind, your will is His will, your spirit is His spirit. "I am crucified with Christ; nevertheless, I live; yet not I, but Christ liveth in me." For your bodies are the members of Christ's body and "ye are the body of Christ." Whatsoever you pray for henceforth, with the consciousness of Christ in you, you will be praying as Jesus called it "in His name," and whatsoever things you ask in His name will be granted.

If you continually watch the action of this great SPIRIT of CHRIST that now fills you, you will begin to learn many things about It. If you treat It as your invisible Friend and Partner, and consult It before you decide anything, you will receive invaluable advice and information. You will find that this Friend is familiar with every move. He knows every nook and cranny of your body and mind. No matter how cleverly your subconscious mind wants to lead you through the avenues of old habits, this great Friend, when given complete control by you, will outwit every move and lead you over dangerous paths to perfect safety. This is the marvelous experience that comes to you after you have actually and literally made your feet like "hind's feet," so that they will completely and utterly follow in the footsteps of Christ.

This Friend within can change disease and wrong conditions in your body. The moment you give Him your unconditional approval to go ahead with His reconstruction work, He at once works through you. But there is one thing about which you must be very careful, and that is that you do not interfere with His action by your worry and anxiety concerning the outcome. To do your work rightly He requires your *absolute trust.* Through the avenue of a peaceful mind only does He do His work.

After you have established perfect faith in the working of this invisible Friend, merely turning over the work to Him, or asking Him to do it, will be sufficient.

Try His help where you are yourself powerless, and see. Suppose you have an enemy whom you have never been able to reach, with whom you are always in more or less peril. Your great Friend will always give you protection as long as you look to Him for protection. Suppose you are going into a movement where there are people who wish to harm or deceive you. Turn the case over completely to your Friend and you will find yourself completely protected. But when you trust in *Him* you must also trust the persons you ask Him to guard you against, for only in your trust in them, who, like you, are also children of God, do you give the matter COMPLETELY to your Infinite Father.

But suppose some one does deceive you, what would you do? Simply look to your Friend and He will bring the adjustment—and with marvelous ease and quickness. The deceiver will sooner or later find it less profitable to deceive you than to help you.

You are now in partnership with the greatest of Engineers. With Him you can do all things. He is your silent partner. He is so silent, that sometimes you will find yourself in danger of thinking that you are the entire firm. But never forget that He organized it, He capitalized it, He is capable of directing it. The articles of incorporation are set forth in the Bible, "Ye have not chosen Me,

but I have chosen you and ordained you." He has com-
missioned you to be His representative in those things
that touch your life, and through you He does His work.

Knowing that Christ has entered and filled you completely, that your very breath is His breath, and your every
good and sincere desire is His desire, sit down and contemplate the deep wishes that come to you after you are
still enough to enter into this holy of holies. Glance over
the list of your desires on the first day, and make a little
readjustment here and there. Then marvel at the beauty
and the power and the possibilities that rest in such wishes when completely surrendered to the will of God. Go
back to the list of blank checks and select out the first one,
and recopy it in large letters in your "hind's feet" notebook. Over and above all of your other little desires place
the desire TO BE FILLED WITH HIM—and see what happens
in the next few days. What a marvelous thing it is to be
able to desire with all your heart and mind and soul and
strength, something as wonderful as this—and how marvelous it is to know that it is possible to receive the fulfillment of your deepest soul's sincere desire!

MEDITATION

Abide in Me, and I in you. As the branch cannot bear
fruit of itself, except it abide in the vine; no more can ye,
except ye abide in Me. Henceforth I call you not servants;
for the servant knoweth not what his lord doeth: but I
have called you friends; for all things that I have heard of
My Father I have made known unto you. Ye have not
chosen Me, but I have chosen you, and ordained you,
that ye should go and bring forth fruit, and that your fruit
should remain: that whatsoever ye shall ask of the Father

in My name, He may give it to you (John 15:4,15,16). (Read John 15.)

PRAYER

O Blessed Christ, enter and fill us and take control of every area of our lives. Our very hearts are Thine; all that we have is Thine. Take us, use us, lead us wherever Thou wilt. We have no fear as long as Thou art our Guide. Amen.

II

Dreams That Come True*

Two gates there are for dreams," said Penelope to Odysseus after his ten years' wanderings had ended. "One made of horn and one of ivory. The dreams that pass through the carved ivory delude and bring us tales that turn to naught; those that can come through polished horn accomplish real things whenever seen."

Whenever a dream comes forth from the ivory gate that is carved and made by man, shaped and twisted by his wish-thinking, his prejudices and half-formed opinions, it always falls to the ground as worthless; but whenever it comes forth from the gate that God has made, the horn that needs no carving or artificial molding, which requires only a little polishing to make it seen in all its native power and beauty—that dream always comes true. I know because I have tried it.

Eighteen years ago I dreamed a dream. It was a dream of taking Jesus completely at His word and placing all the desires of my heart in His hand and letting Him bring them to pass in His own way and in His own time. And my dream came true. This dream, morning, noon, and night, in sunshine and in shower, in work and in play, in joy and in pain, has been the dream I have lived by.

I have put this dream to the most pitiless of tests, both of analysis and of logic, both of life and of experience. I

*First printed in the Winter Number, 1935, of *Religion and Life*.

have applied it to the littlest concerns and to the greatest. I have used it in cases of sickness where doctors gave no hope of recovery. I have used it in cases of hopeless drunkards. I have applied it to individuals and to groups. No matter what the difficulty, no matter how great the hopelessness—everything was changed the moment the dream that was made of horn came into action.

I wrote my dream into a little book, and thousands of people read it. Then came a deluge of letters from people who had shared my dream and found that it was a dream that came true: people who had been sick and now had become well, people who had dreamed of beauty and now were writing best sellers or painting beautiful pictures, men and women who had faced financial ruin and now were starting anew on the ladder of achievement, literally thousands who had been living to themselves alone, who were now looking out upon the world with eyes of new-born men. Statesmen and cowboys, football-players and bishops, actors and explorers, mothers in homes and men in business—there was no group or class that was not represented among those who bore witness to the truth, that our sincere dreams that pass through the gate of horn always come true.

The little book that I wrote twelve years ago was called *The Soul's Sincere Desire*. I believed then, and I believe now, that a soul's sincere desire is a desire that is always fulfilled. Just as the horns which project from the heads of cattle are made and fashioned by God according to the needs of the animals upon which they are placed, so I believe that our sincere desires are placed in our hearts, are molded and fashioned there by the hand of God. An insincere desire, a desire for that which we in our heart of hearts do not really wish, but which, because of our jealous regard for our neighbors or through our desire to keep up with the Joneses, or through the benumbing teaching of an artificial school system, or through the thwarting of an antiquated social order, we have wrongly planted in our hearts—such a desire is carved by our own wish-thinking, it is made of nothing but ivory; and it is such desires that delude and "bring us tales that turn to naught."

Our dreams, in the first place, rise from desires. They are indexes of what in our deep subconscious self we seek and crave. And what a person seeks and craves, other things being equal, is something that is good for him, something which God intended for him to have, provided he can take it in the way that will do no violence to any accepted moral or social code. One deep desire is to sleep when tired, another is to eat when hungry, another is to play, another is to work, another is to love a maid. What tangles the skein is when one would sleep when he should work, eat that which is not his, and love a maid who belongs to another man.

But I did not write this book of *desires, unqualified* and *uncontrolled*. I wrote of *soul's sincere desires*. This immediately changes things, safeguards one against evil, lifts one above wrong. For it is only our little ungrown-up desires that are bad. Every mature desire, every desire that is whole, sincere, complete, and, above all, which acknowledges its relationship to its Divine Maker, is always a good desire. The moment a desire acknowledges its sonship to the soul it becomes a desire for the mutual welfare of all, and joins the little family of virtues which Paul enumerated in his "fruits of the spirit." For the moment a desire becomes a soul's desire it takes its stand alongside Jesus' great commandment, "Love thy neighbor as thyself," and His Golden Rule which tells us that "Whatsoever ye would that men should do to you, do ye even so to them."

The first test applied to the dream of horn as opposed to the dream of ivory is—Does it come from an integrated personality? The simplest way of applying this test is to ask the question, "Is it a sincere desire?"

The second test applied to the dream of horn is—Does it come from a personality that is integrated with God and man? The simplest way of applying that test is to ask the question, "Is it a soul's desire?"

Every desire that meets these two tests, if converted into prayer, is always answered in heaven. When a desire meets these two tests, and not until then, does it qualify to deserve the title of "A Soul's Sincere Desire."

The chief reason for the widespread doubt of the power of prayer is because our civilization, in spite of its being called a "Christian civilization," has produced so few integrated personalities. The only one who completely met this test was the founder of this civilization—Christ Himself.

Our school system has not contributed much toward creating sane, complete personalities. It has, through its standardized processes, repressed personality more than it has released it. Lincoln and Edison were men whose dreams came true because they were fortunate enough to have escaped the "schooling process" altogether, and therefore their dreams were always sincere and always their own. What was their experience, in slightly modified form, has been the experience of all great inventors, great poets, and great geniuses of every age since the beginning of time.

Every great man whose dream came true was first of

all an unrepressed individual who knew and was un-
afraid to know what his honest, sincere desires in life
were. When a man honestly and truly knows a thing, he
believes in it, and when a man believes in a thing it
comes to pass. That is one reason why the dreams that
pass through the gate of horn "accomplish real things
whenever seen."

The wisest man of Greece has probably summed up
better than anyone else this first step in the secret of mastering life in the two words, "Know thyself." How few of
the people in this day and age have learned that lesson.

But this is not the only lesson that a man must learn,
who would find his dreams coming true. Another wise
man, this time the wisest man of Rome, stated the second
step in the secret of mastering life in the two words,
"Control thyself." A dream is not a sound dream, a real
dream, if it cuts counter to the welfare of others or if it
destroys the precious safeguards of society. "So act," is
the ringing categorical imperative of Immanuel Kant,
"that the axiom of thy act may become law universal." In
other words, a desire or a dream, or even a prayer, must
"grow up" and achieve a social maturity before it can
walk forth and conquer the world. That is why the prayer
of the neurotic and of the psychopathic has always had
to linger awhile at the gate of heaven before it could be
allowed to enter. Little baby, pouting prayers go up daily
from thousands of throats; angry, self-assertive, clamoring prayers of the spiritually adolescent are also heard
abroad in the land. All these merit Jesus' gentle rebuke,
"First be reconciled to thy brother, and then come and offer thy gift."

But while Socrates and Marcus Aurelius have thus laid
down the first two laws that govern the integrated, ma-

tured personality through the knowing and the controlling of oneself, it awaited the wisest Man of Galilee to state the third and final law for the mastering of life in the two words, "Deny thyself."

Having found your sincere desire and having brought it under control, and having brought it also into harmony with the highest principles of society, the final act essential for the dream to come into fulfillment is to lose it. The best way to lose it is to give it over completely into the hands of God. Indeed, without this third and final step all other steps are but walking around in circles.

The final test of the true maturity and completely integrated quality of a dream is one's willingness to give it away.

A child who admires the garden seeds but will not remove them from the bright illustrated containers which his father has given him, and whose false cupidity will not permit him to bury them in the cold, damp earth, is, after all, merely a child and we forgive him for his ignorance of the laws that operate in the great garden of God. But the adult who keeps his choice assortment of desires done up in their beautiful dream packages, always ready at hand to exhibit to doting relatives and friends, is to be pitied; and when he gives utterance to his resentment against an "unheeding and unjust Providence that neither hears nor answers prayers," he needs to be taken by the hand and gently taught the primary and kindergarten laws that operate in the realm of the spirit.

When I entered the kindergarten of the spirit and first tried to apply these laws, I found that the effort to lift a desire into the realm of sincerity, and next into the realm of the soul, was no easy task. But, sensing that it was the task necessary for all true prayer, I kept patiently at it until the lesson was learned.

My first prayers, I found, had to be directed toward the finding of my actual soul's sincere desires, and not until I sought them earnestly and passionately did I begin to find them.

And once having found the real things for which I was to pray, and having become convinced, through the preliminary test, that they were things for which I had a right to pray, I proceeded to pray for them. Lest this sound like using God as a mere errand boy to run my errands, let me remind you again that the final and most difficult law in the kindergarten of prayer is giving the whole thing—not only the possession of what you want, but even the process of achieving that possession—completely into the hands of the Father. And by "process of achieving" I mean giving God the right of using any avenue and any agency which He cares to use to bring your dreams into fulfillment in His own way and in His own time.

One way of finding out one's actual soul's sincere desire is to retrace one's footsteps to his childhood, and recall what his honest, sincere life ambitions were at that time. My memory goes back to the time when my cousin and I talked over our life plans together at the tender age of nine. She wanted to become rich and put on style. I wanted to become a writer. At the age of thirty we met again and confessed that neither of us had attained our life's dream. Then, almost simultaneously, we stumbled upon the third and most important law of the dream that comes true. We both learned how to deny ourselves.

As I looked one day at the boys and girls in my creative-writing class it dawned on me that here were greater potential writers than I had ever been. Why cling to my selfish wish to make *myself* a writer? Why not unselfishly devote my energies to helping my students become great writers? And so with the emphasis changed from "self" to "soul," I gave myself to teaching with redoubled faith and energy. Then, in an unconscious moment of pure desire to help another I wrote down some ideas in response to his crying need. "That is too good for me alone," he said. "Why don't you send it to the *Atlantic*?" I acted upon this advice and immediately back came a letter saying, "Send us half a dozen more like it." Thus my boyhood dream came true.

My cousin in the meantime also went through a similar metamorphosis, although in an entirely different way. She also shifted her attention from her outer self to her deep self. Her selfish, sincere desire became a soul's sincere desire. Then one evening she walked across the street, and under an arc light a bug got in her eye. In the corner drug store a tall kindly gentleman drew forth a clean handkerchief and got the bug out. But during the process another kind of a "bug" got in *his* eye. A few months later they were married. Then he broke the news to her that he had a comfortable income and that he wanted her to pick out her own car and "put on style." Thus her girlhood dream came true.

Hard as it is for people to discover their actual sincere desires, far harder is it for them to convert those sincere desires, when once found, into soul's sincere desires. The most difficult situation in which to make this transformation is when those who are very dear to us are on the verge of death. It is very easy at such times to know what our sincere desire is—it is far harder to give that desire over to the greater will of the Father and let it become a soul's desire. But when that great surrender has been made I know of no other field of human need where the results are so irresistible, so unexplainable, and so wonderful.

One day a mother called me over the telephone and told me that her son had infantile paralysis and would I pray for him. Two weeks later she called again, and her heart was in her voice. "Six doctors have held a consultation and have given my boy no hope to live. He has been paralyzed from the neck down for a week. His back has been punctured eleven times. He has a temperature of 105 degrees, and has been having two convulsions a minute for the past four hours. Is there anything I can do?"

"Pray," I replied.

"How shall I pray?"

"Pray, not by asking, but by giving. As you ask you shall receive. But as you give, you also shall receive, and the process of giving at a crisis like this will open your soul more completely than the process of asking. As the tides go out, they will come back. As you give wholly, wholeness will come to you and to those that belong to you. But to give wholly is harder than it may seem. It means that you must give your boy completely and utterly to God. Let God take him into heaven if it is His will— let Him take him and keep him forever, if that is the plan."

"But I want my boy."

"If your boy grew to be a man and was elected a Senator of the United States, would you object to his going to Washington? Would you want him to lose the opportunity for fulfilling the great destiny God has planned for him, just in order to keep him living in your neighbor-

hood so you could have the luxury of seeing him whenever you wished? Heaven is a far more wonderful place
than Washington, and to sit at God's right hand, a far
higher honor than to sit at the right hand of the President
of the United States. You don't know what your boy's life
on earth might be—what suffering and sorrow he might
be escaping by going to heaven at this time, if it is God's
will. Don't let your devotion to your boy become mere
'attachment.' Don't let your mother love become 'smoth-
er love.' Go to your room and kneel down and give your
boy to the Father—to keep or give back, according to the
best plan for the boy."

Presently the phone rang again and a cheery voice
said: "I have given my boy to the Father. I am ready to
accept with radiant acquiescence whatever He wills to do
for my son."

Within two months this boy was perfectly well and
back in school without even a limp to show that he had
been sick.

One after another I have seen children who had been
given up by doctors come back from the threshold of the
grave when the agonizing prayers rising from mother
hearts (and usually from breaking hearts) were transformed, through the miracle of prayer, into "radiantly ac-
quiescent" soul's sincere desires for God's plan to prevail.

I have seen many miracles of healing, but the biggest
miracle in every case occurred in the healing of the heart
of the mother or the father, before the trivial healing of
the body of the child took place.

To make this record complete I must state that very old
people, especially when attacked by cancer, epilepsy, or
insanity, when given completely to the Father, have often

been taken by Him—and sometimes more immediately than they might have been taken had there been no prayer of surrender offered. One must never forget that when one prays the prayer, "Here, Father, take my loved one, and return him to whatever destiny is in Thy plan," one must not be surprised if the Father accepts the prayer at its face value and keeps the one prayed for through all eternity.

My experience with financial problems has been the same as when praying for physical problems. The year before writing *The Soul's Sincere Desire* my wife and I wondered whether our desire for a little crystal radio set—the fad was just coming in—was a right desire. We found that it would cost us exactly $8.70 to buy the little toy novelty, so we made our desire a soul's sincere desire by leaving it entirely to the Father to decide. A few days later two checks, totaling $8.85 came to me from absolutely unexpected sources. We accepted this as a sign from the Father that we were to get the radio set. The third day the little wire antenna for connecting with the stations broke and it cost exactly fifteen cents to replace it—total $8.85.

That winter we had a sincere desire to get out a little printed tribute to my mother, who had died in the fall. Although my share for the publishing of this would be only fifteen dollars, we wanted to be perfectly sure that God would bless us in this undertaking, so we again left the matter entirely to the Father. In the next mail a check for fifteen dollars came from another totally unexpected source.

But why mention these little episodes of money and healing when the great thrilling dramas of the past ten years have been the changing of human souls? I will tell you the reason. These little episodes that pertain to material welfare are *short stories*. Each episode is complete in itself and ends when the material blessing arrives. On the other hand, the unfolding, the awakening, the upward progress of human souls is a continued story. It becomes an epic, which, beginning on this planet, extends like Dante's "Paradiso" on into realms that have no end. Before I could relate these larger sagas, my listeners would first have to remove their shoes—for where we stand would be holy ground.

The chief essential of the dream that comes through the gate of horn is that it be silent. The chief essential of the seed that grows is that it be buried. My most precious seeds of this spiritual planting are still growing. It would be a sort of sacrilege to pull up these plants by the roots to prove that life is in them. My most precious dream-fulfillments are right now attending high school and college, they are in business houses and housewives' kitchens. Some of them are carrying messages of God in unmistakable, irresistible words of power to men and women all over this nation. They are not "finished," they are not ready to be put into a book any more than the history of the United States in the next twenty years is ready to be put into a book.

You may have heard how Dr. George Carver of Tuskegee goes into his laboratory ("God's Little Workshop," he calls it) and prays, and great discoveries come to him. One day I wrote Doctor Carver, until then a stranger to me, and by return mail I received a letter saying, "I was praying that you would write me, when your letter came." So immediately come the answers to some of our soul's sincere desires.

Another great praying soul was George Müller of the Bristol Orphanages. You may have heard of his habit of going into his inner closet and asking God for the financial help he needed for his orphanages, and exactly the sum he required came to him. He said, "When I asked the Father for one hundred pounds, it came; when I asked for a thousand pounds, it came; I am convinced that if I should ever ask for a million pounds it would come just as easily."

I have referred before to Lincoln and Edison as two men who were not "tensed up" by the training of the schools. It has been my observation that all great praying men are simple, relaxed men. Mrs. Thomas A. Edison once said to me, "Mr. Edison's methods are just like yours. He is always perfectly natural and always perfectly relaxed. He feels that all of his discoveries have 'come through him,' that he is but a channel for forces greater than himself."

Always natural, and always relaxed! I do not like to see men work too hard at their prayers. Beware lest the zeal of thy house shall eat thee up. When one strains and labors over his dream he is too often carving ivory and not polishing horn. Don't cut too deeply, don't carve too hard, don't paint the picture too much yourself. Get still awhile, and let God paint it through you. Wrote Gutzon Borglum, "When I carve a statue, it is very simple. I merely cut away the pieces that don't belong there and the statue itself presently comes into view. It was there all the time."

Gutzon Borglum was an artist, George Carver a scientist, George Müller a social worker—but their methods were essentially the same. And what they tested and proved, we too can test and prove.

What are your actual, honest, sincere desires shorn of all inferiority complexes, shorn of all repressions, shorn of all temptations to defense, to compensation, to escape? Spend a week and write them down; erase from time to time the desires you do not really feel sincere about and add others which you find forcing themselves more and more into your consciousness. Half of the people of this nation would find that the list of their desires at the close of the week would be very different from the superficial ones they would put down at the beginning. Water that comes from a pump that has long been in disuse is at first muddy and brackish, but after the surface water has been pumped away, the water from the deeper levels comes forth pure and clear and undefiled. As an actual fact, nine times out of ten, the deeper one goes into his inner soul the more genuine, as well as the more unselfish, his desires will become.

To pray in this way is to pray as a perfectly integrated personality. And remember that the first test of integration is the test of sincerity. *Are you integrated with yourself?* The second test of integration is the test of the soul. *Are you integrated with God and man?* In other words, are your conscious desires integrated with your subconscious desires? Are you walking with "feet like hinds' "? Perhaps the simplest way of summing up everything that has gone before is to say that the chief characteristics of the soul's sincere desire, as opposed to the insincere and superficial desire, are the long look as opposed to the short look, the whole view as opposed to the partial view, the look upward as opposed to the look downward. Let us apply these tests to the desires that are deep within our hearts.

FIRST DAY

WHATSOEVER THINGS ARE TRUE

Write down in your notebook any wish that you believe can meet the test of being a true soul's sincere desire. This week is to be reserved for your own wishes, your own wants, your own desires. Sit down, therefore, and concentrate for once on what you truly want. Make the list as complete as you can. Be as specific as you know how. If you need money to complete a year in college, put down the exact amount you think it will require. If you want an automobile, put down the make and the design, and the color if you can. If you want a job, indicate the exact type of job you want. If you want a house for your family, put down the style and general location. You might even draw the house plan, but *do not* be *so* specific that you pick out your *neighbor's* house, or your *neighbor's* job, or your *neighbor's* automobile.

What capacities in yourself do you want to pray for? Here again be specific. Is it health you want? Greater power of concentration? Greater gift in public speaking? Greater power in making friends? List everything you really and truly want.

Let me tell you why I want you to be specific. These desires are to be "leaders" which, having been sent out, and kept in mind for this week, are to be relinquished completely when the week ends, permitting the Father to amend, change, and correct them, in any way He wishes. But in order to relinquish something you must first *have* it. So begin this week, not with relinquishing, but with a discovery of your desires. Build up the desires faithfully, carefully, earnestly, but according to a sound and spiritual plan drawn from the very Scriptures themselves. And this week we shall let Paul furnish the plan by which you are to draw up your wishes. For seven days you are to write and rewrite these desires, amending them, adding to them, subtracting from them, as the spirit moves you, while you apply each day one or more tests, drawn from St. Paul, to prove whether they are truly soul's sincere desires, desires for which you have the right to ask. Using the seven "whatsoevers" of Jesus, and his three "anythings," write down at least ten new desires. When your list of desires is complete, apply the seven "whatsoever" tests of St. Paul, to see if you have a right to pray for them: "Finally, brethren, whatsoever things are true, whatsoever things are honest, whatsoever things are just, whatsoever things are pure, whatsoever things are lovely, whatsoever things are of good report; if there be any virtue, and if there be any praise, think on these things."

Today let us apply our first test: Are the things you are desiring and praying for true to your own nature? Did you ever realize that it is one of our God-given duties to be a good receiver of things, yes, a good "asker" as well as a good "giver"? Did you ever realize that there are some things for which we *ought* to pray? If an apple tree could pray, its positive duty would be to pray for a crop of apples. An oak tree would fail of its duty if it did not pray for a harvest of acorns. On the other hand you will certainly agree with me that an apple tree should not pray for a harvest of acorns, and an oak tree should not pray for a harvest of apples.

You will agree with me, I am sure, that it would have been perfectly right for Shakespeare to pray to write wonderful plays, and for Columbus to pray that he might reach a new world, and for Edison to pray that he should invent the phonograph, the electric-light bulb, and the moving-picture machine. Think how much poorer the world would have been if these things had not been!

But you will agree with me that it would have been absurd for Edison to have prayed that he should write "Hamlet," or for Shakespeare to have prayed that he should have invented the phonograph. In other words, each one has a right to pray for that which is true to his own nature.

Today look at your notebook and make sure that the desires written there are TRUE to your nature. There are a few things, of course, about which there is no question. Some common basic things are true to all of us. We need, for instance, fresh air, exercise, and nutritious food, the chance to work and play, good friends, and the opportunity to meditate and think. If you lack any of these things, which we might call the Great Common Denominators of all mankind, then you certainly have a right to pray for them. Beyond that, however, we step into a field that requires a great amount of guidance. The first lesson you are to learn this week, in making your feet into "hind's feet," is that it is perfectly right for you to pray for whatsoever you *truly* need, for whatsoever will help you to bring into more perfect expression your true nature. A robin could not possibly desire to swim, and a sunfish could not possibly desire to fly. Nature is always TRUE to type. Prayer, the most natural function to which man has fallen heir, is always true to type. How simple life would be if every person knew exactly to what type he belonged, and therefore exactly for what things he should pray!

This week you must learn how to be a "good receiver." There is an unselfishness that permits you to accept with gratitude and enthusiasm all the riches that are meant for you, and to use them creatively and joyously to bring happiness to yourself and to others. The more things you use that are truly your own, the more you will enrich others—not impoverish them.

A peach tree without peaches because the apple tree does not have them, or the apple tree that refuses to bear apples because the poor elm tree cannot have them, is not helping others, but is obviously robbing mankind. The great actor who is so "unselfish" that he will not act, and the great musician who will not play, and the great writer who will not write, and the great executive who will not accept responsibility—are all robbing mankind of great riches. Likewise, the man who actually should have a car, and refuses to accept it, is not kind to the salesman, to the manufacturer, or to the factory laborer who must keep his job.

A certain amount of courage and confidence in your prayer is a spiritual virtue. Remember that God is as true as mathematics. If two plus two make four, all the argument and debate, yes, all the persecution, in the world will not alter this unchangeable fact. If it is true that your nature is to write poetry, all the scoldings of parents, scoffings of friends, or criticisms of teachers will not be able to prevent you. Pray with courage and confidence and your prayer will be answered according to God's plan for you.

Now make an analysis of yourself and your true needs. Write down your deepest desires that meet this test of trueness. Make the list specific. Think of your "desire nature" as it actually is—as a tree anchored in the soil of the love of God. Let the trunk of the tree be the Kingdom and its righteousness. Above, the trunk is subdivided into three main branches, designated as Persons, Ideas, and Things. Draw a picture of this tree in your notebook, and on each branch make a numbered list of things, persons, and ideas you want. Be very specific. Write down the names of persons you would like to have for friends—or the type of persons you feel that you have a right to have as friends. Then list the *things* you would like to have. If a trip to Europe, write the exact journey you would like to take, mentioning the countries and the chief cities you would like to see. If a college education, the name of the college and the course you would like to take. This may sound silly and strange, but remember that all of this is subject to the veto of God—for you always add the provision, "If this is TRUE for my nature, I want it, otherwise Thy will, not mine, be done." Remember that you have a duty to fulfill to the world in serving it to the height of your nature, as much a duty as the bird which sings its beautiful song.

In your quiet time remember that just as surely as every snowflake that falls has a perfect design, and no two designs are the same, so within the folds of your being lies a design. Ask the Father that this divine inner plan of your life may stand forth revealed to you as it should be, unfolding in perfect sequence and perfect order in such a way as to bring the greatest good to the greatest number. You have drawn a tree. If your wish for life is an acorn, your tree will be an oak. If your wish is for a peach stone, the tree will be a peach. Nothing can change your nature. Nothing can change the nature of your prayer, and, finally, nothing can prevent the fulfillment of your prayer if it is true to your nature, and a sound reflection of your inner soul.

MEDITATION

The Lord is nigh unto all them that call upon Him, to all that call upon Him in truth. He will fulfill the desire of them that fear Him; He also will hear their cry and will save them. The Lord preserveth all them that love Him (Ps. 145:18-20). They that worship Him, must worship Him in spirit and in truth (John 4:24). Ye shall know the truth, and the truth shall make you free (John 8:32). Therefore love the truth (Zech. 8:19). (Read Gen. 13:14-18.)

PRAYER

Our Father, as the sheep know the shepherd's voice, may we know the true call of the Good Shepherd whenever He speaks within our soul. Amen.

SECOND DAY
WHATSOEVER THINGS ARE HONEST

The surest means we have of finding out whether a thing is true for our nature is to ask ourselves whether we honestly desire it. It seems unreasonable to imagine that an acorn could ever honestly desire to be anything but an oak tree, or that wheat could possibly desire to be corn. No robin ever desired to swim, and no sunfish to fly. A setter dog desires to hunt, and a spaniel to swim. The test of honesty, then, is a very important test. Our success in applying it depends upon our power to reduce ourselves to our elemental simplicities—to turn and become as a little child. A child is always honest. A child never fails to state his real desires. He is frank and open about it. You may depend upon him. I feel sure that our Heavenly Father appreciates childlike candor in all of us. As parents are guided in their selection of Christmas presents when their little children make lists of what they want for Christmas, our Heavenly Father in His infinite power is guided by our prayer lists in determining what He shall send us.

Do we really want what we think we want? Suppose that a committee waited upon me and told me that they wanted me to run for Governor of Minnesota, explaining to me all the honor and glory of it, and how my name and my picture would be in the paper, and so on and so on. I would immediately ask myself whether I honestly wanted that office. Would I be willing to make welcoming addresses to doctors' and dentists' conventions? Would I be happy in trading offices and extending patronage to my votegetters? Would I—But why continue further? Would not this work actually destroy my true work—the opportunity I crave for teaching and for writing and for speaking on themes that are my true message to give to the world? Suppose that an agent came to sell me a hundred magazines. Would I honestly like to have that many around, tempting my time from other reading? When a man is turned down by a girl and he immediately marries another, is he doing this because he is honestly in love with her or is he merely seeking compensation for lost pride, lost peace, lost comfort?

Beware lest we ask for things out of spite, out of jealousy, out of envy or out of pride. Put down only the things which you are absolutely sure that you honestly desire, and then look at them every day for a week, testing them from every angle. When you are positively *sure* that you honestly want them, then you can confidently give your request to the Father, knowing that when your honest wish and His honest wish coincide, nothing can prevent perfect fulfillment. More than half the job of praying is completed when we are sure that we truly and honestly desire that for which we pray.

How did Columbus come to discover America? Because deep down in his inner soul he had a tremendously urgent, honest desire. How did Shakespeare happen to write great plays? Because down deep in his inmost soul he also had a deep, honest desire. How did Edison and J. J. Hill achieve what they achieved? Because they were acting to the best of their ability to bring to pass that which they *honestly* desired to bring to pass.

Our soul's sincere desires are prophecies of what we truly should have, should be, and should possess. We should be true to our own honest desires. They are, other things being equal, about the only things we have by which to test our real life purposes. Of course we occasionally fool ourselves. Sometimes we imagine that we have a soul's sincere desire, whereas it is only an attempt to imitate John's desire. Sometimes we desire just because it is fashionable, or because our family insists that we should. Today sift out the true desire from the false desire, by the simple test of "whatsoever things are honest." If it is "honest" we have a right to pray for it.

Now go over the prayer list as worked out yesterday, and apply each desire to this test. Remove some items from the list and add others, as the spirit guides you.

MEDITATION

Blessed are they which do hunger and thirst after righteousness; for they shall be filled (Matt. 5:6). For He satisfieth the longing soul, and filleth the hungry soul with goodness (Ps. 107:9). (Read I Sam. 17:32-52.)

PRAYER

Our Heavenly Father, O Thou who "openest Thine hand and satisfiest the desire of every living thing," keep us as simple and clear as the boy David who refused the armor that was not his own. Keep us as honest and sincere as a little child. Show us the real desires of our heart, and, having found them, keep us true to them that they may manifest through us according to Thy heavenly will. Amen.

THIRD DAY
WHATSOEVER THINGS ARE JUST

Today go over the things for which you have asked, and see if they meet the test of absolute justice to your fellow man. Be sure that you are not asking for that which will take something from another. Are you praying for a particular job which some one else holds, and who would have to be discharged before you could receive it? Are you praying for a certain buyer for your property, whether it is for his best interest or not? Pray, rather, that a person who can find great happiness in your property will buy it. Pray that if it is in God's plan, you can have a home as lovely as the home you especially admire.

If your list meets the test of justice to your fellow man, go over it again to see if it is just to your God. You hear a great deal about waiting for your ships to come in. Ask yourself, did you ever send any ships out? If you have toiled without proper pay for many years, if you have created wealth for others, or brought comfort or joy to others for which you have never been adequately recompensed, and have done it cheerfully, then indeed you have sent ships *out*. Then you may properly wait with *expectancy* for ships to come *in*. Vash Young received big returns in his business, but his chief thought was not on the returns. He first planned his work so that he could give half of his day to helping others without thought of recompense; he took pains not to see that his ships came in—that is God's business—but to see that his ships went *out*—that was *his* business.

Perhaps it is not wealth or money for which you have asked, but a trip to Europe. Then have you studied Europe, its history, its scenes? Are you properly prepared to derive full measure from such a trip? Remember that Emerson said we bring back from Europe only what we take to Europe. Are you prepared to pay the price in values for that which you hope to bring back with you from Europe? If you are, then you may look with expectancy to the gift of the trip to Europe. Or, have you prayed to become a great orator? If so, have you paid the price in practice and study, and are you willing to continue to pay the price as the days go on? If you have, then you may justly pray for that gift, not otherwise. In praying for a debt to be paid us, are we overlooking a debt that we owe another?

Go over each prayer and ask, Have I justly earned—through toil, sacrifice, and service—the right to pray for this thing? Am I taking what is my own, or does it actually belong to another? Am I ignoring any just duty I owe to others in departing on this journey? Am I encroaching upon anyone's privileges, property, or personality, in asking this of God? In asking that love be given to me am I neglecting to give my love to those who have a right to expect it from *me?* IS THE PRAYER I ASK ABSOLUTELY JUST?

MEDITATION

And if a man also strive for mastery, yet is he not

crowned, except he strive lawfully. I have fought a good fight, I have finished my course, I have kept the faith: henceforth there is laid up for me a crown of righteousness, which the Lord, the righteous Judge, shall give me at that day: and not to me only, but unto all them also that love His appearing (II Tim. 2:5; 4:7,8). (Read Ps. 1.)

PRAYER

We thank thee, Father, for the great security and safety Thou hast granted us in living in a world governed by law, where the stars keep in their courses and the law of gravity and the law of the tides abide forever. Help us to walk according to Thy divine laws of the soul. May we ever keep Thy statutes, and honor Thy covenants, and hold fast to Thy commandments. May all that we think and do be just and righteous altogether. Amen.

FOURTH DAY
WHATSOEVER THINGS ARE PURE

The most essential thing for a perfect prayer is perfect love. Love is the most wonderful thing in the world. Of all the virtues it is the force that draws us and holds us closest to God. Let us keep this love stream as pure as possible from the elements that might defile it. The word *pure* is a tremendously big and all encompassing word. Just as *sin* means anything that separates us from God, so impurity is anything that blocks the channels of heavenly love. Let us keep this love as God-like an experience as we possibly can. The first thing that blocks this flow of love is possessiveness. The moment we love a person merely for gratification or personal satisfaction, we are separating ourselves from God.

Whenever we use a man or woman, not as an end in

himself, but as a means to another end, our purpose is not absolutely pure. Purity should begin in the home. A marriage which is founded for the purpose of sex gratification and nothing else will defeat its own end. Only as we lift sex, and witness it as a glorification of God, as a means of making man less selfish, and less carnal, are we seeing it in its true light. Not until we bring in adoration and reverence are we completely safe with sex.

But there is also impurity in looking at persons as mere means of increasing one's wealth. In fact, a man who marries a woman for her money is as impure in his way as the one who marries her to gratify mere physical passion. A dictator who sees people as mere cannon fodder, an employer who sees his workmen as mere "hands" to increase his output, libertines who see women as mere objects for their lust, are all equally impure in the sight of God.

Do our souls' sincere desires meet this test of purity?

Perfect purity was defined by Jesus in two commandments: First, "Love thy neighbor as thyself." Second, "Whatsoever ye would that men should do to you, do ye even so to them."

"Treat each individual as an end in himself, and never as a means only." If we could meet the highest test of Kant's Categorical Imperative, this would be a wonderful world. Jesus it was who showed the world the infinite value of each individual soul. Every person, even the meanest outcast, is made after the image and likeness of God. In each person we meet, if we look far enough into him, we shall see the face of Christ. That is true reverence—and reverence is the only final test of true purity of mind. Not until we revere everyone we meet, as a perfect being in a perfect world, governed by a perfect God, can we truly say that we are pure in heart. When we attain that purity of heart, said Jesus, we shall see God. And, conversely, we might say that only those who see God in every person they meet are truly pure in heart.

Does your soul's sincere desire meet this test of purity?

If you pray for wealth that requires sweatshop labor to produce, then you have no right to pray for that wealth. If you pray for happiness that requires anyone to lower his ideals to achieve this for you, you are using another as a means to an end, and your pleasure is not pure. But if your soul's sincere desires are based upon the recognition of the infinite value of every human soul, give them to the Father with the assurance that they will be heard in heaven.

MEDITATION

The wisdom that is from above is first pure, then peaceable, gentle, and easy to be entreated, full of mercy and good fruits, without partiality and without hypocrisy (James 3:17). See that ye love one another with a pure heart fervently (I Pet. 1:22). Unto the pure all things are pure (Titus 1:15). Blessed are the pure in heart: for they shall see God (Matt. 5:8). (Read Ps. 51.)

PRAYER

Our Heavenly Father, "Thou art of purer eyes than to behold evil and canst not look upon iniquity." Bring us so close into Thy blessed presence that we shall be divested of all that is unlike Thee. May we so reverence every individual human soul that we may make the world a purer and sweeter place in which to live. Amen.

FIFTH DAY

WHATSOEVER THINGS ARE LOVELY

Henry Wright, the revered saint of Yale University, has given four tests of guidance which have been faithfully followed by thousands of people, the Oxford Group being the most recent and outstanding example. The four tests are: Is it Honest? Is it Unselfish? Is it Loving? Is it Pure?

In these studies of Paul's WHATSOEVERS we have already applied the tests of honesty and purity. In our study of truth and justice we have applied the test of unselfishness. We are now to apply the test of love.

The word lovely is a wonderful word. It suggests the sense of beauty and love rolled up together: the beauty that stirs one to a love of a thing, and the love that thrills one with the beauty of it. Sometimes we do loving things awkwardly, clumsily, and in ways that do more harm than good. But when we do a loving thing beautifully, gracefully, harmoniously, what more can we ask? Pray, then, for beautiful things, knowing that this praying for beauty is not vanity, pride, or selfishness. Is there vanity in God when He gives us beautiful sunsets, flowers, and lakes? Is He not making His love more manifest in bringing this beauty to gladden our eyes and hearts? We too have the right to make life for others sweeter and happier and more beautiful. We have a right to pray for greater beauty and happiness to shine from our faces, greater eloquence to clothe our speech, and a finer grace to govern our actions. Yes, there is no sin even to pray for more beautiful garments to clothe our bodies, and lovelier homes in which to entertain our friends. The more beauty we demand, even in such outer things as these—provided we can afford them—the greater demand will be made upon workmen to create beautiful things out of beautiful materials, making the whole world a busier, happier, lovelier, and more heavenly place in which to live.

And the wonderful thing is that the test of beauty is one of the tests of the goodness and trueness of a thing as well.

Anything that is very true, is always very good, and if we look into it deeply enough it is always very beautiful. A maple leaf, true to its own nature of line and fiber, is always a good thing, and always a beautiful thing. A snowflake is beautiful, but only when true to its own pattern and design. A bridge in a graceful arch is beautiful, and its very grace and beauty are proof that it is good and strong and true to its purpose.

Let us set our hearts today on beauty. Pray that beauty and loveliness may enter every corner and phase of your life. Pray for manners that are gracious and lovely; vision yourself conversing with charm, addressing an audience with lovely words, writing your ideas of goodness and truth in beauty and loveliness of phrasing. Hold fast to this vision of loveliness, and your very face will become like a window—more transparent—to let the beauty of God shine through.

The final and highest test of loveliness is love itself. What is more lovely than love? What is more beautiful than love shining through the face and eyes? What is more graceful and poetical than the movements and gestures of a body overflowing with pure, high love?

Do your prayers meet this test of loveliness in its finest expression? Are they filled with beauty? Are they filled with love? If so, they are what you have a perfect right to ask your Heavenly Father to give you.

MEDITATION

Love suffereth long, and is kind; love envieth not; love vaunteth not itself, is not puffed up, doth not behave itself unseemly, seeketh not her own, is not easily provoked, thinketh no evil; rejoiceth not in iniquity, but rejoiceth in the truth (I Cor. 13:4-6). (Read Ps. 107.)

PRAYER

Our Father, help us to see the true loveliness of love. May we seek it as "the greatest thing in the world." May we express it all the day long in the most beautiful ways of which we are capable, so that it may bring gladness to the hearts of all. Amen.

SIXTH DAY

WHATSOEVER THINGS ARE OF GOOD REPORT

From now on you are to believe in answered prayer. Henceforth, you are to live in the constant expectancy of GOOD tidings. You probably know many people who live constantly in the expectation of bad tidings. Some folks literally enjoy bad health—they are always saying, "I am sick, I am unhappy, I am miserable." You are to be one who says, "I AM WELL, I AM HAPPY, I AM FILLED WITH JOY." Speak the word in a spirit of faith, and the atmosphere of radiant happiness and optimism will shine through you.

But, you say, anything I hate is hypocrisy, make believe, playacting; all of this sentimentalism and Pollyanna stuff makes me sick! Splendid! I heartily agree with you, and with everyone who demands absolute honesty in his optimism, or his pessimism, or any other "ism" he has. Any counterfeit, spurious make-believe gladness, proclaimed with a smirk instead of a smile, with a grimace instead of a grin, is positively deadening. What we want is *real optimism*—or nothing. To take one of the great tragedies of literature—such as Macbeth—and transform its tragic outcome into a heroic triumph for the two murderers, and let them "live happily ever after," would be maudlin sentimentalism and would destroy the purging effect such a tragedy should have upon people. But if we changed—not the ending, but the beginning— by having Macbeth filled with the spirit of Christ's love, instead of with the fever of selfish ambition, then we would have a RIGHT to bring a good report of how he and his lady lawfully succeeded to the Scottish throne, and how the two lived happily as king and queen "ever after."

In the same way you have the right to change some of the impending tragedies in your own life and in the lives of your friends, if you do it, not by sentimental attempts to change the ending, but by a vital, creative attempt to change the beginning. Alter your purposes, your intentions; turn them upward, make them large enough to take in God and your fellow men, and the bad report will become a good report.

After this week of self-analysis and of self-discipline, you have a right to expect a good report on your list of prayers. In other words, you have earned a real optimism if you have obeyed the rules of the game. If your wishes and prayers are based upon the truth of your own nature, if they are lovely, and filled with love and beauty, if they have all these things, then you have no right to believe in bad luck, or in bad tidings, either for yourself or for anyone else.

Having met the other tests in Paul's famous list of "whatsoevers," carry henceforth an expectant optimism in looking forward to the answers to your prayers. By expectant optimism I refer to the type of optimism of the little girl who, when she heard that her parents were going to church to pray for rain, ran back home to get an umbrella. George Müller, of the Bristol Orphanage previously referred to, is an outstanding example of one who prayed with expectancy, because he knew that he had met the other tests that Paul has given for prayer.

Norman Harrison in *His in a Life of Prayer* tells how Charles Inglis, while making the voyage to America a number of years ago, learned from the devout and godly captain of an experience which he had had but recently with George Müller of Bristol. It seems that they had encountered a very dense fog. Because of it the captain had remained on the bridge continuously for twenty-four hours, when Mr. Müller came to him and said, "Captain, I have come to tell you that I must be in Quebec on Saturday afternoon." When informed that it was impossible, he replied: "Very well. If your ship cannot take me, God will find some other way. I have never broken an engagement for fifty-seven years. Let us go down into the chartroom and pray."

The captain continues the story thus: "I looked at that man of God and thought to myself, What lunatic asylum could that man have come from. I never heard of such a thing as this. 'Mr. Müller,' I said, 'do you know how dense this fog is?' 'No,' he replied, 'my eye is not on the density of the fog, but on the living God, who controls every circumstance of my life.' He knelt down and prayed one of those simple prayers, and when he had finished I was going to pray; but he put his hand on my shoulder and told me not to pray. 'Firstly,' he said, 'because you do not believe God will, and secondly, I believe God has, and there is no need whatever for you to pray about it.' I looked at him, and George Müller said, 'Captain, I have known my Lord for fifty-seven years, and there has never been a single day that I have failed to get an audience with the King. Get up and open the door, and you will find that the fog has gone.' I got up and the fog was indeed gone. George Müller was in Quebec Saturday afternoon for his engagement."

MEDITATION

How beautiful upon the mountains are the feet of him that bringeth good tidings, that publisheth peace: that bringeth good tidings of good, that publisheth salvation; that saith unto Zion, Thy God reigneth! (Isa. 52:7). It is a good thing to give thanks unto the Lord, and to sing praises unto Thy name, O Most High: to show forth Thy loving-kindness in the morning, and Thy faithfulness every night (Ps. 92:1-2). (Read Ps. 104.)

PRAYER

Our Heavenly Father, we thank Thee that we live in a world where light is in control and where darkness is but the absence of light. Help us to keep our eyes upon the sunshine and not upon the shadows, upon the reality of Thy Love and not upon the counterfeits of the Wilderness. Oh, that men would praise Thee for Thy goodness and for Thy wonderful works to the children of men. Amen.

SEVENTH DAY

IF THERE BE ANY VIRTUE, AND IF THERE BE ANY PRAISE, THINK ON THESE THINGS

After a farmer plants wheat he does not lie awake nights worrying lest radishes come up. He knows that it is the nature, or we might say the *virtue*, of wheat to grow wheat. It is the virtue of acorns to grow oak trees. And it is the virtue of prayers that are based upon that which is true, honest, just, pure, lovely and of good report, to come into fulfillment. Such a fulfillment is in accord with the inevitable unfoldment of all moral law. We do not have to argue or get excited or perspire over trying to make four plus four equal eight. It is the virtue of such a combination to become eight. It is the law of mathematics, irresistible and inevitable as the tides.

In the same irresistible, tidal way, trust to the inborn virtue residing in these laws of the true, the honest, the just, and the pure in your list of desires, and give them completely to God. Relinquish them into His hands, and go off and leave them. Do not worry about them, do not even pray for them for the next few weeks. Give them as completely as the farmer gives his wheat to the soil, after the soil has been properly plowed and harrowed. Later on, when the weeds begin to come up, we may have to get into these prayers with a cultivator and re-mellow the soil of our faith a bit, but now, go off and leave them entirely.

Remember that we are dealing with something more spiritual, more heavenly, than the planting of wheat. We are dealing with the planting of prayers. This is the most sacred, the most beautiful, the most wonderful planting, that anyone can render for himself or for the world. It is so wonderful that before we leave it we must do one thing more.

When a farmer plants wheat he waits for the harvest, and after the harvest is over and the grain is in the barns he observes a national Thanksgiving Day on the last Thursday of November, when he and his friends gather together and give thanks for the harvest. That is all very well when planting material things. But when planting spiritual things—prayers, instead of wheat—we should not wait until *after* the harvest to hold our Thanksgiving Day. We should hold it in advance.

Paul does not use the word Thanksgiving. He used the word Praise. Praise goes one step beyond Thanksgiving. Thanksgiving usually is withheld until the blessing is received. Praise, on the other hand, does not wait for results. It speaks out of turn with abandon, with alacrity, with joy and enthusiasm. It does not wait to see whether the prayer is answered before it speaks. It dances and sings before its Maker in the pure love of His presence.

If your prayers this week have met the tests of truth, honesty, justice, purity, love, and "good tidings," leave them in the hands of God, and turn your thoughts now to praise. If all of your prayers should be answered, would you not feel like praising God? If so, why wait until He has answered them, why not start the praising right now? Do you always wait until a thing has been delivered from the store before you pay for it? Have you not sometimes had the virtue and the grace to pay for a thing before it is delivered? I know that the thrifty person pays in advance only those whom he can trust to deliver the goods in first-class condition and to give full value for the price. But with whom are you dealing now? Do you not realize that you are dealing with the most perfect, the most just, the most merciful, the most generous, the most wise, the most farseeing One who ever did business with mankind? Why should one hesitate to pay *Him* in advance?

Start the praise you wish to give Him, not in words, but deep down in your heart. The praise you wish to give must be in spirit and in truth. Give Him credit for all that you have, all that you do, all that you are, and all that you hope to be. "Every good gift and every perfect gift is from above, and cometh down from the Father of lights, with whom is no variableness, neither shadow of turning." Rejoice and praise, rejoice and praise, and again I say, rejoice. For the Lord thy God is good.

MEDITATION

O give thanks unto the Lord; call upon His name: make known His deeds among the people. Sing unto Him, sing psalms unto Him: talk ye of all His wondrous works. Glory ye in His holy name: let the heart of them rejoice that seek the Lord (Ps. 105:1–3). (Read Ps. 67.)

PRAYER

Our Heavenly Father, we thank Thee for all Thy loving mercies to us. We thank Thee for friends. We thank Thee for health. We thank Thee for guiding our ways and directing our paths. We thank Thee for endless, countless, priceless blessings awaiting us in the future, which depend only upon our worthiness. Make us worthy of Thy love, for with Thy love all riches are ours. Amen.

III

Prayers That Are Answered

There are two ways of praying for others. One is the John the Baptist way; the other is the Jesus way. One is by law; the other is by grace. "From the days of John the Baptist until now the Kingdom of Heaven suffereth violence, and the violent take it by force." But this violent, forceful way of praying, by the use of the law on the human plane, cannot compare with the gentler way of praying by the grace of God, on the heavenly plane. "Verily I say unto you, among them that are born of women there hath not risen a greater than John the Baptist: notwithstanding he that is least in the Kingdom of Heaven is greater than he."

The method of John, where strong men would take the Kingdom of Heaven by force, is where the person who prays, concentrates his thoughts upon the friend he would help, and by strength of thought forces the trouble to leave. The method of Jesus, on the other hand, ignores the trouble and sees only the Father and His Kingdom, knowing that before a mind so completely filled with God all trouble vanishes away just as darkness vanishes in the presence of light. Jesus made this clear when He said, "Seek ye first the Kingdom of God and His righteousness; and all these things shall be added unto you." This entails no work, for the Father, not we, does the work; whereas the other method requires an immense amount of work. One who uses the John the Baptist method is as exhausted when he is through as after an ordeal; whereas the one who uses the Jesus method is more refreshed after his hour of prayer than when he began. This accounts for the fact that Jesus so often arose before dawn and went into the mountain to pray, an exercise which did not drain His strength, but regenerated it.

But while the Jesus method does not require much work in the way of DOING things, it does require a tremendous amount of work in the way of BEING something.

John the Baptist's method assumes that we are completely separate from our brother, and the only way by which we can reach him is by setting up vibrations in the ether by intensive and "concentrated mental work." We are like icebergs floating on a trackless sea, according to this conception, with no organic connection with one another, moving according to no divine purpose or plan, wherever wind and current carry us. This conception is beautifully symbolized in Lorado Taft's *The Loneliness of the Soul*, where figures are grouped around a pillar so

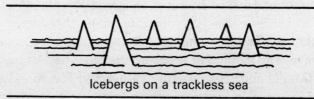

Icebergs on a trackless sea

they cannot see each other, but only with their outstretched hands can they barely touch each other. John was experiencing this loneliness of the soul when he sent to Jesus from prison, asking, "Art Thou He that should come, or do we look for another?"

One who uses the John the Baptist way of prayer must be a strong man mentally and physically, well versed in the law of telepathy and mental therapeutics. For that is exactly what this type of prayer is—sublimated telepathy. The telepathic wave, according to scientists, is just above the Marconi wave—a finer, subtler sort of vibration, but vibration, nevertheless. This way of getting results, when reduced to its simplest form, is usually accomplished by repeating affirmations over and over again. These are repeated as urgently and emphatically as possible in order to force others to accept the statements. This is kept up for many minutes, sometimes for many hours, and at the end of that time the praying person is exhausted. Only a strong man indeed could take the Kingdom of Heaven by force in this way. Coué made great use of it. He taught his disciples that if they repeated to their subconscious mind every morning, twenty times, "Every day in every way I am getting better and better," they would actually get better. Luther Burbank made occasional use of this also. When he wanted to see his sister, who lived in another town, he did not write her, he merely *wished* that she would come, and she would take the next train.

Centuries of application of this form of prayer have proved, beyond all question of doubt, that it is a real and effective method which often produces results. But it is not the highest form. It is not pure spirit. It is on the plane of psychic vibration which lies on the borderland between spirit and matter. Perhaps when we have advanced farther along the line of bringing our physical and spiritual researches together, we shall be better able to define it.

Let me point out here a few of its limitations, which Jesus' way of prayer does not have.

First, as mentioned before, it requires an immense amount of work. Second, working in the "no-man's-land" of the psychic, rather than in the realm of pure spirit, bad thoughts and evil motives may "leak in" and deflect the pure purpose of the prayer. In this case the results, naturally, will also be bad. Jesus was accused by the Pharisees of doing this when they said He did these things by the power of Beelzebub. By Beelzebub they meant that which, in the Middle Ages, was called witchcraft, or black magic, and what today is called hypnosis. Jesus instantly refuted this accusation by saying, "If Satan cast out Satan he is divided against himself . . . but if I cast out devils by the Spirit of God, then the Kingdom of God is come unto you."

Third: The results are not alway permanent. Indeed, the only time the results of this method *are* permanent is where the patient believes strongly: (1) in God, or (2) in the power of love, or at least (3) in the existence of a "Friendly Universe." Careful checking up of the cures wrought by Coué proved that the only cures that remained permanent were among the people who believed in an Infinite Power in one of these three forms.

And what is Jesus' way of prayer? Jesus Himself has very carefully described the difference between His method and that of John's in the first chapter of the Fourth Gospel. Nathanael, surprised that Jesus was able to read his thoughts while he was still sitting under the fig tree, exclaims, "Rabbi, Thou art the Son of God; Thou art the King of Israel." To which Jesus replies that if he thinks it is wonderful that He could use the John the Baptist method of insight and read his thoughts, he does not begin to know the greater wonders that he is going to see. For he is going to be lifted to a heavenly insight where he "shall see heaven open, and the angels ascending and descending upon the Son of Man."

Now the entire difference between Jesus' and John the Baptist's methods of prayer is revealed by two words in the first chapter of the Fourth Gospel. John the Baptist is called the *Voice*; Jesus is called the *Word*. Moreover, the Voice is in the *wilderness*; the Word is with GOD. Just as great a difference lies between the law of the jungle and the Law of God, as lies between a *word* and a *voice*. Both are used in communications of truth between one soul and another, but a *voice* is a communication viewed from the *outside*; a *word* is a communication viewed from the *inside*. One is the shell; the other is the heart.

There is also a world of difference between a *wilderness* and GOD. A wilderness is where everything and everyone is *lost*; God is where everything and everyone is *found*. A wilderness is where everything is separate from every other thing; God is where everyone is united with every other one. As far apart as the law of the jungle is from the Law of God, even farther apart is the *Voice in the wilderness* from the *Word with God*.

In a wilderness all we can hear is a *voice*. Indeed, we are fortunate to hear that. When a man is lost in the jungle, the greatest good he looks forward to is to hear a voice which may lead him out. But when he is in his Father's Home, then he is not content merely to hear the Voice; he wants to hear distinctly what the Voice is saying, he wants to catch each precious word. John's prayer is a pathfinder's voice announcing a trail that will make the way straight back from the wilderness. Jesus' prayer is a Son's voice, confiding his secret wishes and deepest love into the heart of a loving Father. The entire evolution of prayer, from its simplest, most primitive form to its deepest, most intimate culmination, is merely the transforming of prayer from the Voice shouting in the wilderness to the personal, loving Word spoken into the ear of God.

Now let us look into the inner mysteries of prayer as Jesus taught it to his disciples. His most revealing explanation came when He said, "I am the vine, ye are the branches: he that abideth in Me, and I in him, the same bringeth forth much fruit, for without Me ye can do nothing. . . . If ye abide in Me and My words abide in you, ye shall ask what ye will, and it shall be done unto you. . . . Herein is My Father glorified, that ye bear much fruit."

This glorious revelation of our oneness with Jesus, and with the Father, and—through this union—this assurance of answered prayer, is the greatest truth in all the universe. It is so overpowering in its implications, so difficult to understand, so incomprehensible to our finite minds, that it baffles all attempts to diagram or explain. Perhaps the clearest way to make it graphic to our eye is this poorly wrought diagram:

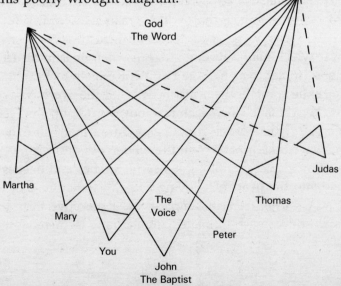

The Vine and the Branches

Jesus said that we are all branches and that He is the vine, by which He implies that we are all branches of our Father. For He added, "In that day ye shall know that I am in the Father, and ye in Me and I in you."

Not only are we all branches of the Father, but all the branches join the vine at the same place—and that place is the place of Jesus Christ. "I am the Way," said Jesus. "No one cometh to the Father but by Me." In the most unique way of all history, He combined the consciousness of God and the consciousness of man. Jesus stood all through His life at the point where humanity and divinity meet. We call this unique position where He stood, the Christ consciousness. The word "consciousness" did not happen to be in the Israelite vocabulary in Jesus' day, so He used another word instead, a word which in that day comprehended all that "consciousness" implied, and even more—the "Name." "Whatsoever ye shall ask in *My name*, that will I do, that the Father may be glorified in the Son."

Prayer with Jesus is very simple. You take your own or your brother's need deep into your heart, and identify yourself with it. Then, forgetting your brother and yourself, as best you can, and, above all, forgetting your trouble, turn completely in thought to God and rise into that high consciousness of oneness with the Father, through the consciousness (or name) of your oneness with Christ, and having risen to that high place, you pray until the Peace of God comes upon you. Then your prayer is answered.

But before you rise to this state of peace and oneness, you have to go through the "trap door" of the soul—the door that has held you so many years out in the wilderness. You will notice in the diagram on the previous page, that Mary and Peter have their "trap doors" open, while Martha and Thomas do not.

This door was called by John the Baptist, "Repentance"; and by Paul, "dying to self." According to Jesus, "the meek," "the humble," "the poor in spirit," "the persecuted," "those who turn and become as a little child," are the ones who will find the secret key that unlocks this door into the Kingdom of Heaven. Jesus summed it all up when He said, "He that loseth his life for My sake shall find it."

Strange to say, the word *helplessness* seems to sum up these words better than anything else—*helplessness* and *trust*. If you would open your "trap door" that leads to Heaven, trust utterly in the love of God and sink back, in your feeling of utter helplessness, with perfect willingness to be helpless. Rest in your meekness with perfect willingness to be meek. Rest in your emptiness with perfect willingness to be empty. It is your very helplessness that draws God's infinite help; it is your emptiness that opens all heaven's infinite resources to fill you.

The Trap Door of the Soul

The way to open the door, in other words, is to empty out all of your tensions. The sins that grow out of an exaggerated sense of self are, to the soul, exactly what tensions are to the body. They prevent the normal flow of the healing circulation, they check the recuperative forces that are ever at work in God's eternal universe. Fear is perhaps the greatest tension—a greater separative force from God than many of the greater sins. Self-consciousness, especially when expressed in self-pity, or self-conceit, is one of the biggest blockers of all. Hate is the most mighty of all the hindrances; hate toward a single individual can block *every* door to God. Lust, greed, and vanity have also strange ways of blocking doors, until they are converted into their opposites of love, generosity and aspiration.

Having opened the door which lets you step from the wilderness of self into the house of God, all you need to do is to mount the stairway of love or peace or goodness, into the very presence of the Christ. Then in His presence (which is the same as saying in His name or consciousness) whatsoever you ask for will be done. Then it is that "ye shall see the heavens open, and the angels of God ascending and descending upon the Son of Man."

When you try to help a friend, his "trap door" must be open as well as yours. He too must be rid of tensions, he must be filled with meekness, trust, and love. If he shares with you in this effort to open the doors of heaven, if he has faith in God, and if he loves and trusts you as an instrument of God, then all you need to do is to take him and his need into your heart and give him completely and utterly to God.

I usually love the person I pray for to the extent of feeling a real concern—so deeply do I love him. But my love must be a high, unselfish love, a love that lifts me above all petty results, especially above any rewards that might come to me. I must love him, not for what I can get out of him in praise or money or pride—I must love him for himself. Unselfish, unself-seeking love is the elevator that will lift one most quickly into the highest level of prayer. The moment you step into this love you have stepped into the greatest power there is—a power that lifts you and all of your friends to the abode where God eternally abides. For God is Love. And when you love in this high sense, you automatically rise to the highest story of the Cathedral of Prayer. You enter into a realm of oneness with God and with the souls of all mankind. At this point you will find that you and your friend have become one.

Then, thinking neither of your friend's need, nor even of him personally, but seeing him as a child of God, a perfect being in a perfect world, governed by a perfect God—let him fade out of mind while God alone fills all the space that he is occupying. And where God is there is no need of any kind, no sickness, no poverty, no crime. Continue in the stillness that comes to you when you have reached this stage, until this stillness becomes a "peace that passeth understanding." The moment this peace comes to you something has happened, something very wonderful, in the outer world as well as in the inner; something to your friend as well as to yourself. For, remember, in this high state of consciousness you and your friend are spiritually one.

The first year I stumbled upon this form of prayer, one Saturday evening, I suddenly felt a great feeling of oppression—as if some one were trying to reach me on the John the Baptist level of prayer, some voice crying in the wilderness, trying to reach heaven by force. I prayed blindly that evening—for something, I knew not what—and received very little sense of peace in return for all my pains. The next morning I awoke with the same discomfort of mind, and prayed again, this time achieving peace, but only to a very slight degree.

That Sunday evening I prayed with a little group of believing friends, and this time a great peace came to me. The following morning a college girl came to my office and said, "Did you get my message Saturday night?" I replied: "I certainly got somebody's message. What was it all about?"

"I went to my home town for the week-end," she said. "My brother took me riding and we stopped at the home of a young couple we knew, and found that their little baby had double pneumonia and was not expected to live. I asked to be allowed to pray for her, and went into the room alone. When I lifted my eyes from my praying and looked at the little baby, it appeared so terribly sick that I became panic-stricken and cried out to you for help. I called your name aloud. Did you hear me?"

"Is that where all the commotion came from Saturday?" I exclaimed.

"I called our friends the next morning," she continued, "and the baby was slightly improved."

"Did you call them Sunday evening?"

"No, I left in the afternoon. Why?"

"If you had called up in the evening, you would have found the child completely out of danger."

"How do you know?"

"Because of the great peace that came to me."

And sure enough, the next morning a letter came, telling her that the child had safely passed the crisis Sunday evening, and they had dismissed the trained nurse that very night.

Later in the year I was speaking in the city of Detroit when, one evening, I read that a resident of that city was to be hanged the next morning in Illinois for a crime that he and his friends claimed he had not committed. His wife, a devout Catholic, was asking through the papers for anyone who believed in prayer to pray that her husband should be spared. I went to my hotel and prayed for him. But how could I love a man with a love that passeth understanding, when I had never seen him? How could I make his problem my problem and take him deeply into my heart and carry him with me up into the holy of holies in Christ's name? I recalled that he had three little children and a wife who would never see him again. I had a wife and three children back in St. Paul, and I knew how they would feel if they were never to see me again. This gave me a sense of identity with him and gave me the power to take him into my heart and make his problem mine.

I prayed that, if guilty, he should go to the gallows with resignation in his heart, or, if innocent, that he might somehow receive the miracle of a reprieve. Then I prayed for peace—a peace, not for him, but for myself— my larger, loving inner self. And at exactly eleven o'clock deep peace came to me and I fell asleep. The next morning I awoke late, and before I was through shaving, the religious editor of the *Detroit Press* came to interview me. I apologized for my late rising by telling of my prayer for the condemned man the evening before, and how peace did not come to me until eleven o'clock.

"At exactly eleven o'clock," he replied, "the Governor

of Illinois, where he was awaiting execution, sent him a reprieve."

Over and over again have my prayers been answered in this startling way, but they come most easily when I *know* the person for whom I pray, and easiest of all when I deeply love him. In fact, I have here recited two of my most difficult experiences in prayer—where in both cases I was praying, as one might say, in the dark.

I mentioned before that you must make your friend's problem yours, that you must feel concern for him, a concern that sometimes amounts to a real fear or sorrow for him. At the tomb of Lazarus "Jesus wept," you remember. And those about Him said, "Behold, how He loved him." But Jesus did not continue weeping. He dried His tears on the remembrance of peace.

"But is not fear or sorrow a hindrance to prayer?" some may ask. To this I reply, "No, if you do not hold to your sorrow or fear."

I have an illustration that will make this clear.

When beating a rug in the winter-time, I take it out upon the snow and beat it till most of the dust is gone. Then I throw handfuls of our dry, crisp, Minnesota snow upon it until the very warp and woof are filled with it. Then I take a broom and sweep it and keep on sweeping until all of the snow is swept away. At this stage I no longer look for dust, I look for snow, knowing that the snow is very much easier to see against the dark background of the rug.

When I pray I let my loving concern for my friend fill every fiber of my being. Then, knowing that in my inner mind it is much easier for me to watch my own concern than the trouble of my distant friend, and knowing that my concern is lovingly interwoven with his trouble, I

concentrate upon sweeping out the concern, knowing
that when that is completely gone, the trouble of my
friend is also completely gone. Wonderful, isn't it—to
take yourself for an occasional house-cleaning in order to
help your friends like that? And do not all of us need to
be taken for a little spring house-cleaning occasionally?

I am not afraid of fear. I am certainly not afraid of sorrow. And I am positively fond of concern—loving concern. The only thing I am afraid of is the holding on to
them. So when I pray for my friend, and feel a great concern for him arise in my heart, I am glad, for I know that
the first step in successful prayer has been taken. Then I
get out my little broom of prayer and immediately start
sweeping away, not the trouble or problem of my friend,
but my own concern—yes, my own fear and my own sorrow for him. Nor do I stop until I have swept it all
away—every bit of it, completely out of the corridors of
my consciousness. How can I tell when I have swept
these things away? Very simply. By the great peace that
comes in their stead. Once I find this peace within my
own soul, which reveals that all fear and concern is
swept out of my own consciousness, and I know that my
friend's trouble is gone.

This is the secret of my own power in prayer, and herein lies a deep mystery, a mystery to myself and to my
friends, a mystery, that, until now, I have found it very
difficult to explain.

And the mystery is this, that the heavens open and the
angels ascend and descend—angels of loving concern ascending, and angels of heavenly peace descending—angels with infinite healing in their wings—angels that literally bring God's Kingdom into manifestation upon
earth as it is in heaven. Then one knows what Jesus

meant when He said to Nathanael: "Because I said unto thee, I saw thee under the fig tree, believest thou? Thou shalt see greater things than these. . . . Verily, verily I say unto you, hereafter ye shall see heaven open, and the angels of God ascending and descending upon the Son of Man."

FIRST DAY
THE PRAYER OF MEEKNESS AND FAITH

I. Meekness.—We are now ready to take the twelve stairways that lead to the upper chamber of answered prayer. Any one of these, when climbed with the "hind's feet" of the Spirit will lead us to the high places, where all of our problems will be solved. But he who has mastered all twelve will be especially able, not only to solve his own need, but also the needs of many struggling souls. If one should spend a lifetime mastering just one, his time would be well spent. We should certainly be willing to spend one week on the twelve.

Let us first climb the stairway of *Meekness*. Nine of these stairways are Paul's "fruits of the spirit," but I am not taking up these fruits of the spirit as Paul listed them, rather as Jesus would have listed them. Jesus always put Meekness first. "Blessed are the poor in spirit: for theirs is the kingdom of heaven."

Meekness is the key by which the door of prayer is made easy to open. The humble and poor in spirit find it easy to pray, for true prayer consists merely in opening the door and letting Jesus come into our hearts. The first step in prayer, as explained before, is simply letting go of our tensions, so that Jesus can have unhindered entrance into our souls.

Thus prayer is like a song, with its cadences, its overtones and its undertones, its rhythms and its infinite beauty. And just as music has its octaves, so prayer has its octaves, and the power of our prayer depends upon how true we can sound the high notes in our singing. It is also like a mountain trail with a series of ledges. The first appearance of Meekness to many is on the lowest ledge of *Humiliation*. At least that is where many of us meet it first. Few of us are willing to bow down and take the humble place until outer events—misfortune, failure or disgrace—force us down. This ledge of Humiliation leads us up to the second ledge of *Repentance*.

Here something creative happens. The doorway to heaven opens and some of the healing power of God enters in. But we are still a long way from the heights of heaven, for Repentance is a looking back, not a looking forward. Repentance, however, leads us to the ledge of true *Humility*, which is a marvelously cleansing and healing stage. From here it is a short step to the ledge of *Meekness*, which carries with it a marvelous, invisible power—a power which prepares one for the next step, a very momentous one for any of us, that of *Surrender*.

Surrender, like Repentance, is an act, not of the will only, but of the entire being. Surrender and Repentance carry us through two gates—one opening backward, the other forward. One takes us out of the bad, the other carries us into the good. One opens with the key of silver, the other with the key of gold. One closes the door on life's negatives, the other opens the door on life's positives. When we have stepped completely through the gates of Repentance and Surrender, we have stepped into the Kingdom of Heaven.

We have now reached the high level of *Selflessness*, where we are willing to have God enter us, and fill us completely, taking entire control; and when He has taken over that entire control we enter the next stage, that of *Transparency*, where the light of God's truth and wisdom flows through us unobstructed, lighting all those around us. But wonderful as it is for God's *wisdom* to shine through us, there is still a higher stage—the stage where His *power* can shine through us. For this there is required such a complete emptying of self, that the only term adequate is *Incandescence*. On this high plane all of the infinite power of God's unlimited Niagara can come flowing in. Edison could not let the full power of Niagara light our houses until he was able to empty all the atmosphere completely, from the interior of a fragile little bulb of glass. God never completely turned on *all* of His power in any single being, until a Man of Galilee so completely erased Himself out of the picture that He could say, "The Father that dwelleth in Me, He doeth the works."

                                                INCANDESCENCE
                                          TRANSPARENCY
                                      SELFLESSNESS
                                  SURRENDER
                              MEEKNESS
                          HUMILITY
                      REPENTANCE
                  HUMILIATION

Behold, now, the octave which lifts our song of prayer. Behold, the steps that lift our feet like the hind's feet to our high places where all of our prayers are answered. Let us assume that we have already started at the bottom, that *Humiliation* has led us to *Repentance*. Let us quickly journey upward, through *Humility* and *Meekness* to true *Surrender*, and step into the glorious realm, the heavenly land of *Selflessness.*

Let us get still—very, very still, and enter the marvelous experience of being entirely *Transparent*, and utterly *Incandescent.* While we may not be able to maintain a continuous abode in the realm of *incandescence* or *transparency*, or even *selflessness*, while we may not be able to abide there for even one hour, we may occasionally attain such heights for at least one moment. Even the disciples, you remember, could not keep watch with Jesus one entire hour, but fell asleep by the way. So, our higher consciousness will often fall asleep; but if and when we do attain that moment of *transparency* or *incandescence*, know that in that moment God is answering our prayer.

II. Faith.—Faith makes a perfect partner with Meekness. Meekness says, *"I cannot do it."* Faith says, *"God can do it."* So alongside of the pillar of Meekness we should erect the pillar of Faith, knowing well that if we trust ourselves to the rungs extending between them, we shall have a perfect ladder into the Kingdom of Heaven.

Faith is a combination of thought and emotion, so perfectly integrated with the will that one can act upon it. The culmination of perfect Faith is perfect action. Let us start at the lowest point of emotion, and trace the steps to the highest point of Faith.

The lowest emotion that living creatures ever experience is a sensation. A moth has no will and no mind, but even a moth can experience a sensation. It flies into a flame and gets a sensation of burning. It flies into it again and gets another sensation of burning. But it is totally incapable of taking those two sensations and multiplying them together and producing a perception. The best it can do is to add one sensation to another sensation, and still remain on the one-dimensional level of sensation.

A dog, however, when it walks into a fire and gets the sensation of burning, and the next week slips against a red-hot stove and gets another sensation of burning, has the power of *multiplying* these two sensations together and producing a perception. But while he has risen into the two-dimensional realm of perceptions, the dog cannot, by any twist of his doggish logic, multiply perceptions together and create conceptions. He cannot produce a steam-engine, a warship, or sign a declaration of war or a treaty of peace.

Man alone has the power to multiply perceptions together and create conceptions, and by that means he has created our modern civilization. The reason why our modern civilization is in such a mess today is because man is content to remain in the realm of conceptions. While he has clear-cut conceptions of the injustice and futility of class hatreds, and of race hatreds, for instance, he does not do anything about them. While he has had proven to him, over and over again, the futility of war, like the moth in the flame, he continues to rush into war on the slightest pretext, until it begins to appear that he will perish at the hands of his own vast inventions.

If a man would escape from his present dilemma, there remains for him one step more, a step that will carry him as far above his present selfish, insane level of living as an ordinary man is above the level of the dog and the other brutes, and as far as the dog is above the moth and the other insects. And that step is for man to take two or three of his conceptions, say, for instance, the foolishness and futility of war, and *multiply* them together, by some secret spiritual process of celestial cube root, and lift himself into the heavenly realm of *Realization*.

George Müller took two or three promises in the Bible where God gives assurance of His care for orphans and for those who cry out to Him in need, and multiplying these, he stepped into the realization that God meant what He said. Then with that realization he asked God for help for his orphans, and over seven million dollars came to him.

George Fox and William Penn took two or three commands of God regarding "Resist not evil," "Forgive your enemies," and "Turn the other cheek," and accepted them not as conceptions, but as realizations. During the 150 years of Indian uprisings in Colonial history there were more Quakers exposed to Indian attacks than any other group, and yet not a hair of their heads was injured.

But it is a great big jump from the conceptual level to the Realization level, and few are able to make it with one or two quick leaps. Rather it is a gradual process of

---

                                          KNOWING
                                    ◄REALIZATION
                              CONVICTION
                        FAITH
                   TRUST
              BELIEF
        CONCEPTION
   OPINION

---

climbing. Early in our childhood we turn our sensations and perceptions into *opinions*. Opinion, therefore, is the first round of our ladder. *Opinion*, after being carefully examined and thought upon, becomes a *Conception*: As the *Conception* grows firmer and clearer in our mind we accept it as a *Belief*. Next comes *Trust*. A man may *believe* a parachute will open, and still not *trust* himself to its weight. When he arrives at *Trust*, he has reached the stage where thinking begins to be converted into action. When one trusts his *Belief*, he is at the threshold of true *Faith*. When Faith becomes settled and permanent we call it *Conviction*. Then dawns *Realization* and we begin to function in the undimensional realm of heaven. Finally we reach the state of absolute *Knowing*, and we step out upon the promises of God with the same assurance that we step upon a train or enter into a neighbor's house.

Now let us put these pillars of Meekness and Faith together and use them as a ladder to climb into the Kingdom. Step into the realm of absolute *Selflessness, Transparency,* and *Incandescence*, and wait for God to enter in and fill our Being. At the same time let us step into per-

The Kingdom

MEEKNESS	FAITH
INCANDESCENCE	KNOWING
TRANSPARENCY	REALIZATION
SELFLESSNESS	CONVICTION
SURRENDER	FAITH
MEEKNESS	TRUST
HUMILITY	BELIEF
REPENTANCE	CONCEPTION
HUMILIATION	OPINION

MEEKNESS   *FAITH*

fect *Conviction, Realization* and *Absolute Knowing* that God can fill us and can take control of every area of our lives. Then in a state of peace and quietness let us give ourselves and our friends—all our problems and needs—completely and wholly to the Father, and KNOW that He will care for us in His own way and in His own time.

MEDITATION

Trust in the Lord with all thine heart; and lean not unto thine own understanding (Prov. 3:5). (Read Luke 7:1-10.)

PRAYER

Our heavenly Father, empty us of self and fill us with Thee. Amen.

SECOND DAY
THE PRAYER OF LOVE AND PEACE

I. Love.—Faith lifted to its highest level is *prayer*. Love lifted to its highest level *is God in manifestation among men.* For God is Love. To climb the ladder of Faith to the high realm of Realization brings us into the realm of continuous prayer; to climb the ladder of Love to the high realm of Oneness will bring us into the realm where we shall "dwell in the House of the Lord forever."

The first rung in the ladder of Love is mere *Liking*, a very feeble and lukewarm step away from the ground of cold selfishness and indifference. The next step is that of *Attachment*, which is a form of selfish friendship that binds more than it sets one free. A step farther on is *Affection*, which carries one just a little farther away from selfishness, but still does not free one entirely from jealousy and possessiveness and the emotions that bind.

True liberation only comes when you step into true *Friendship*. This in turn, grows and deepens permanently in *Comradeship*. You are on the threshold of heaven itself when you step through the doorway of high *Love*, in all of its spiritual connotation.

                                    ONENESS
                              REVERENCE
                         LOVE
                   COMRADESHIP
              FRIENDSHIP
           AFFECTION
        ATTACHMENT
LIKING

Lift your *Love* still higher and you enter the realm of *Reverence*, and on into the highest loyalty of all—absolute *Oneness*. Your friend's welfare has now become your own welfare; his interest your interest. What hurts him hurts you. When all lower grades of affection surrender allegiance to this higher type of affection you are ready to pray the prayer that will be answered. At this point your prayer becomes actually your friend's prayer, and your love your friend's love.

We hear a great deal about the value of Prayer Groups. Did you ever appreciate the value of Love Groups? Did you ever realize what miracles could happen if a little group of your friends would get together once a day, or even once a week, and *Loved* everyone that needed their help. Get your family, or your group of friends, together some day and try it.

Instead of making out a "prayer list," make a "love list" of those who need you, those who need God, those who need help of any kind, and *love them*. Turn in thought to each one in turn, and love him without stint and without limit. See him as a son of God—then there is *reverence* in your love. Identify his interest and welfare with yours, then there is *oneness* in your love. Do not think of this love as a personal, individual affair, beginning with yourself and ending with yourself, or even beginning with the group and ending with the group. Think of it as a great impersonal force, the love of God Himself, pouring through you as the ocean pours through the Straits of Magellan, blessing all those in the path of its healing flood.

Live in this ocean of love, immerse yourself in it, let it fill you even to the very finger tips—not the merely sentimental kind, or the cold impersonal kind, but the real, irresistible, heavenly kind that flows through you from the Heavenly Father, who so loved the world that no literature written can give full expression to it. Then pray for the persons you dearly love. Pray until this love merges into a perfect peace.

II. Peace.—After you have lifted your friends into the heart of God through loving them selflessly as described above, all you need to do is to wait until peace enters your soul, and you will know that God's blessing has come upon them.

The chapter preceding this week's study describes the value of peace in such detail that there remains but one thing to make clear at this time. Some people cannot realize why peace can produce such powerful results in prayer. Some people can see small difference between the feeling of heat felt by the moth and the feeling of peace felt by a man. The only answer to this is that the one is a *sensation*, the other is a *realization*. There is as much difference between a sensation and a realization as there is between the insect that crawls and the prophet who prays. A sensation is the *effect* of some larger cause. A realization is a *cause* that creates effects. The one who lives by sensations is a slave to Fate; the one who lives by *realization* is a master of Fate.

If I had health and wealth and friends I would have peace of mind, says the one who believes that peace is caused by something else. But I have seen people lose their peace of mind because they were overwhelmed by the temptations of too much wealth; I have known others who, like Charles Lindbergh, had everything but peace of mind because of the importunity of the multitude of their friends. On the other hand, I know of very many persons who had nothing but peace of mind, and their peace and serenity, like a great magnet, drew to them loyal friends, happy employment, and abundant health. Do not forget that peace, which is a realization, is a *cause*; the peace that is a sensation is an *effect*.

This realization of peace, this great creative peace, this

                                                        PEACE
                                                  SERENITY
                                            TRANQUILITY
                                       STILLNESS
                                 CALMNESS
                           REPOSE
                  RELAXATION
           REST

---

peace that passeth all understanding, does not come without effort. We must earn the right to this peace by climbing faithfully from the lower levels, where it is not much more than a mere sensation, up to the heights where it is a high realization.

Let us turn back to the list of friends whom you have been lifting with your Song of High Love, and start the Song of High Peace for the complete solution of their needs, as you slowly climb the stairways of Peace. Beginning with the sense of *Rest*, relax all of the tensions of your muscle-bound body. Then *Relax* your mind and soul of all of its soul tensions, dropping out all greed, avarice, lust, jealousy and fear. Find *Repose* in some beautiful promise of God, some beautiful Christlike soul, or, better still, see the Christ soul of the one for whom you are praying. Step up through *Calmness, Stillness*, and *Tranquillity*, to high *Serenity*, until you have reached the high level of the *Peace* that passeth all understanding. Then our song of peace has, like our song of love, ceased to be a mere song, and has turned into a prayer. Abide in this peace that passeth all understanding, and in this love, for a little while, and all of your friend's needs will be met. Whenever you carry your friend up both these stairways, first of love, second of peace, all of his problems will be ended.

MEDITATION

God is Love, and he that dwelleth in love dwelleth in God, and God in him (I John 4:16). Thou wilt keep him in perfect peace, whose mind is stayed on Thee: because he trusteth in Thee (Isa. 26:3). And the peace of God, which passeth all understanding, shall keep your hearts and minds through Christ Jesus (Phil. 4:7). (Read John 11:32-44.)

PRAYER

Our Father, we take our loved ones and all those who need us deeply into our hearts and there we give them completely to Thee. May Thy peace, the peace which passeth all understanding, rest with them, bringing Thy perfect fulfillment to all their needs. Amen.

THIRD DAY

THE PRAYER OF GOODNESS AND GENTLENESS

I. Goodness.—The pathway to heaven most commonly preached to us in church, and urged upon us by parents, is the pathway of Goodness. How good are you? Looked at from the heavenly point of view, we are all sons of God, but looked at from the earthly angle we all have much of the little imp in us at times. Let us see how far up the stairway of *Goodness* we can rise toward the Kingdom of Heaven.

The lowest step is *Innocence.* Every little child starts with that. Even when he puts his fingers in the jam, or spills the syrup-pitcher, we are gentle with him because we know that he does not have any evil intent. But as he grows older he learns the difference between right and wrong, and attains what we call the sense of *Rectitude.* This leads him to appreciate the quality of *Honesty* in all of his dealings. *Justice* is one step higher, because it requires more impartial weighing of motives—which, when attained, leads on to the high level of *Virtue.*

Virtue is Innocence grown up, Innocence that has been proved and tested, Innocence that can withstand the attacks of all evil. It carries strength and courage, from the Roman word from which it is derived. But it still looks downward toward man, using man's strength and man's courage. When we reach *Goodness* we find a word de-

PERFECTION

RIGHTEOUSNESS

GOODNESS

VIRTUE

JUSTICE

HONESTY

RECTITUDE

INNOCENCE

rived from Godliness, that brings us strength from heaven. *Righteousness* is called by some Right-use-ness, because it implies the right application of goodness and virtue to the practical affairs of this life.

Last of all is the highest step, that of *Perfection*. This, you say, you cannot ever attain. But in the few moments given to devoted prayer, see if you cannot manage to drop out *all* of your evil thoughts, forgive *all* of your enemies, step above *all* earthly desires, for just one moment, and for that moment, at least, experience *Perfection*. To attain that high pinnacle, even for one moment, brings you into the place where all of your prayers are answered.

II. Gentleness.—But Goodness is not all for which we should strive. There is something greater than Goodness. Many people seem born good. They have calm, even dispositions; they are rarely provoked. They seem impervious to the ordinary temptations. They have been surrounded by good influences from their childhood up. And yet, with all of that Goodness they are very uncomfortable to live with. Being so good themselves, they

COMPASSION

MERCY

SYMPATHY

CHARITY

GENEROSITY

KINDNESS

GENTLENESS

TOLERANCE

have become critical and impatient with those who are not so good. How often it is that the person who is not so good, or who, at least at one stage of his life was not so good, is the most compassionate and tolerant toward the erring ones, and the most fervent in the saving of sinners.

So, before we go farther, let us climb the stairway of *Gentleness*.

Our first step is *Tolerance*, which is a negative term, an absence of criticism, prejudice or disdain. Then to *Gentleness*, which is positive, but mild and unassertive. This leads us to *Kindness*, which lifts Gentleness into a feeling of kinship with others. *Generosity* is a great word suggesting both Gentleness and Kindness toward those to whom we are not obliged to be kind. *Charity* is the widening of this Generosity into still larger fields. *Sympathy* is an actual "suffering with" those who suffer, and weeping with those who weep. It is Kindness and Gentleness springing from the deepmost heart. *Mercy* is the giving of our sympathy and our self to those who are in our power or to those who do not deserve it—a giving in a high spiritual way. *Compassion* is also a "suffering with," but I place it

above Sympathy, because the gospel-writers have associated it with the name of Christ. It is Sympathy, with
Christ added. It is the highest point that I can reach on
this stairway.

Let us take these twin pillars of *Goodness* and *Gentleness*, and stand them upright, side by side. Then let us
join them with a series of eight cross-bars, connected by
the eight virtues in each. Starting at the lowest rung of
this double ladder, we find that Innocence looks out upon
the world with Tolerance. The next step reveals Rectitude, softened by Gentleness. Then Honesty expresses itself in Kindness and Justice is softened with Generosity.
Then Virtue sweetens itself with Charity and Goodness
with Sympathy. The highest rungs reveal Righteousness
giving power through Mercy, and Perfection made perfect through Compassion.

When you learn how to climb this ladder which com-
bines the Goodness which shuns sin, with the Gentleness
that loves the sinner—this ladder which unites the Righteousness that abhors evil with the Sympathy that em-
braces the one who creates evil—then your prayer is
heard in heaven. One reason why Jesus is so loved by
mankind is because He is the great outstanding example
of one who was sinless, and yet was compassionate with
those who did sin.

When the good and the gentle are combined in a soul,
there you will find a saint. Jesus' two greatest parables
describe such saints—the good Samaritan and the compassionate father of the prodigal son. Never did the
world need them so much as she needs them now. Pray
that God will raise up such saints. Pray humbly that He
will make you a compassionate father or a good Samaritan whenever the need demands; there is no prayer you

could ask that would benefit mankind more than that. Be just as good as you can be on the inside; then look out with all the compassion of your soul upon those who are erring and faltering on the outside, and even though you may not pray a word, your goodness and gentleness will be a living prayer.

Here then we find another irresistible team in prayer that deserves to stand beside the other two. Meekness and faith are irresistible in opening the door to God's power when praying for our own needs; love and peace are irresistible in opening the door of God's power when praying for others who are in sorrow; goodness and gentleness are irresistible in opening the door of God's power when praying for others who are in sin.

MEDITATION

And God saw everything that He had made, and, behold, it was very good (Gen. 1:31). For every creature of God is good, and nothing to be refused, if it be received with thanksgiving: for it is sanctified by the word of God and prayer (I Tim. 4:4,5). He hath showed thee, O man, what is good; and what doth the Lord require of thee, but to do justly, and to love mercy, and to walk humbly with thy God? (Micah 6:8). (Read Matt. 5:43-48.)

PRAYER

Our Father, may we be good, may we be without blemish, faultless in Thy sight and in the sight of men. But, above all help us to be merciful even as Thou art merciful to those who fall by the wayside, gentle to those who err, kind to those who are weak, doing justly, loving mercy, and walking humbly with our God. Amen.

Fourth Day

THE PRAYER OF PATIENCE AND JOY

I. Patience.—With the combined forces of *Meekness, Faith, Love,* and *Peace* behind your prayer, you will find that it is well-nigh irresistible. For the kind of faith we have been talking about has not been mere wish-thinking, and the love we have been discussing has not been sloppy sentimentality, nor has the peace been a mere Pollyanna optimism. On the contrary, they have been something as firm and indestructible as the Brooklyn Bridge or the law of gravity. In other words, we have been discussing a *creative understanding* faith, and a *creative understanding* love, and a *creative understanding* peace. When we add to these the irresistible power of a *creative understanding patience,* you will find that your prayer has become an irresistible force of God. The self-pitying patience of defeat, and the self-deceiving patience of escape are far different from the creative patience of an understanding soul.

So today look at the things that have hurt you in the past, and forgive the person who gave the hurt. There is nothing more regal, more kinglike, yes, more Christlike, than the magnanimity of the person who forgives more than society required him to forgive. It is hard to forget conditions that have cheated us out of a part of our life. Now look at these conditions, right in the face—look squarely at your failure to secure a college education, your illness that left you weaker than others. Look with Edison at his deafness, with Milton at his blindness, and with Bunyan at his imprisonment, and see how their creative understanding patience converted these very misfortunes into good fortunes. Michelangelo went to Rome to carve statues, and found that the other artists had taken over all the Carrara marble—all but one cracked and misshapen piece. So he sat down before it and studied with infinite patience its very limitations, until he found that by bending the head of the statue here, and lifting its arm there, he could create a masterpiece. Thus the boy David was produced.

Let us sit down in front of our very limitations, and with the aid of creative patience dare to produce, with God's help, a masterpiece. Let us forgive our limitations, forgive the people who created them, forgive the events that brought them upon us. A great forgiveness is itself the Greatest Masterpiece of God; so great is it that, just give it a chance, and it will create other masterpieces in time. The most exquisite of perfumes is produced from the fragrance of crushed roses when they have been trod upon. The finest, most perfect essence of the spirit, the power behind our most creative actions, and our most irresistible prayers is the power that comes from converting "ashes to roses"; it is the power which can "restore the years that the locusts have eaten."

I have found in my experience that the one who has come through the deepest tribulations, or who has been beset with the greatest limitations, when once he has risen above them, and has found an inner peace and calm, is invariably the one whose power is most far-reaching in prayer.

Sometimes an answer to prayer is delayed. Our creative patience reveals that this is because God has some larger training and discipline for us than we know. Sometimes when we are focusing our attention upon some great service we would *do*, God is focusing His attention upon some great personality that we should *be*. It is always a greater service that we render through our *being*, than through our *doing*. It is always a greater honor to be called upon to *be something* than to be called upon to *do something*. Just as it takes a month to produce a squash, and a century to produce a redwood tree, so it requires a day or so to *do* something where it takes a lifetime to *be* something.

The stairway of *Patience* often begins, with most of us, at the low stair of *Passive Acceptance*, or of mere *Resignation*, but it is often a flabby resignation filled with despair and without hope. Add a touch of resolution and determination, and *backbone* takes the place of flabbiness, and *Resignation* becomes *Endurance*. We may still be haunted with self-pity, or be peevish with our neighbors, until *Endurance* is transformed into *Forbearance*. The next step is *Forgiveness*, which takes all evil out of that which has oppressed us, and enables us to rise conqueror above it. Our *Endurance* now becomes *Fortitude*, which is one-fourth physical courage and three-fourths moral courage, the true badge of all of the heroes of the Cross. *Long-Suffering*, in its Biblical sense, suggests a saintly quality of uncomplaining fortitude in the presence of suffering that

---

PATIENCE
LONG-SUFFERING
FORTITUDE
FORGIVENESS
FORBEARANCE
ENDURANCE
RESIGNATION
PASSIVE ACCEPTANCE

---

purifies one of all dross. In the mint at Washington the gold is kept in the burning crucible until it becomes so pure that the Director can see his face reflected in it. He who has been in the crucible of *Long-suffering* until he has attained the *Patience* that passeth all understanding, will reflect in the light of his countenance, the radiant face of Jesus Himself.

II. Joy.—Patience is the light that comforts and guides us in the time of darkness. Joy is the full-orbed light of day that drives all the darkness into oblivion. When patience and joy are combined, the effect is tremendous. When Michelangelo, for instance, not only *forgives* his fellow sculptors for using all of the best marble, but actually *rejoices* that he is limited to only one piece, as it enables him to concentrate all of his efforts upon it, then he is sure to produce a masterpiece. Miracles occur when, in the very midst of darkness that tries one's patience, one can turn on the full-orbed light of joy.

Let us now look a little more deeply into the spirit and essence of joy. The roots of all true joy, we shall find, are fastened in love; the leaves and blossoms of it soar high into the light. True heavenly joy is love with this light added. It is love that sparkles, that radiates, that penetrates. It is love that will not be put off, that will not be quenched. It shines until all opposition breaks down before it. Joy is the expression of love by the subtle language of indirection. When a tired father comes home after a hard day's work, and his little five-year-old son says morosely that he loves him, the words do not carry the weight that is conveyed by another little son who says nothing about love, but who claps his hands and dances with joy when his father turns in at the gate.

That is why joy, founded on unselfishness and love, is

more beautiful that love alone. It is love that cannot hold itself within bounds. Joy leaps and cavorts with its very excess, an excess that simply has to overflow and fill everyone else besides. Moreover, joy is proof that love is present in a specifically contagious form. It is so irresistible that it will not stay within bounds. It insists upon shining forth, and radiating to all those within reach. After Jesus had said, "Ye are the salt of the earth," meaning love, he quickly added, "And ye are the light of the world," meaning joy.

                                        BLISS
                                    ECSTASY
                                JOY
                            HAPPINESS
                        CONTENTMENT
                    DELIGHT
                SATISFACTION
            PLEASURE

Let us rise to the place of this high light of *Joy*. The lowest rung of this ladder is the *Pleasure* which we experience following a good dinner or a pleasant game. We rise to *Satisfaction* when a little higher desire is fulfilled, but it is still, usually, a selfish desire. When we receive an unexpected gift we leap out of ourselves for a moment, with *Delight*, but still the roots of the experience go back to self. *Contentment* carries us to more peaceful heights because more selfless. *Happiness* carries us one step higher, for it requires that we share our Contentment and Delight with others. But not until we pass through the doorway of *Joy* are we completely in the presence of the

Christ; for Joy is Jesus' word. He never talks about happiness, or delight; he talks only of *Joy*. "These things have I spoken unto you, that my *joy* might remain in you, and that your joy might be full." *Ecstasy* completes what delight began. It takes one *completely* outside of oneself, immersing one in that which is infinitely greater and more perfect than this little mundane world. *Bliss* is a compound of joy and blessedness, and blessedness is only found in heaven. Blessed, like joy, was frequently on the lips of Jesus, and when both words are combined we find the bliss that is experienced in the heart, whenever it transports us at once into the threshold of heaven.

Patience and joy, when combined, make a beautiful song, one the high tenor, the other the low bass. When harmonized, and not "flatted," they could well be called the "Victory Song of the Soul." Let us climb these celestial octaves to heavenly notes and hold them all day long.

MEDITATION

Wait on the Lord: be of good courage and He shall strengthen thine heart: wait, I say, on the Lord (Ps. 27:14). The Lord is good unto them that wait for Him, to the soul that seeketh Him (Lam. 3:25). And not only so, but we glory in tribulations also: knowing that tribulation worketh patience; and patience, experience; and experience, hope: and hope maketh not ashamed; because the love of God is shed abroad in our hearts by the Holy Ghost which is given unto us (Rom. 5:3-5). (Read Ps. 40.)

PRAYER

Our Father, we do not pray for easy lives; we pray to be stronger men. We do not pray for tasks equal to our powers; we pray for powers equal to our tasks. Turn our disappoint-

ments into Thy appointments. May we create from our very limitations, achievements to do Thee honor. May we turn ashes into roses, turmoil into peace, and patience into joy. Amen.

FIFTH DAY

THE PRAYER OF INSPIRATION AND SELF-CONTROL

I. Inspiration.—Anyone who has climbed these Ladders of the Soul faithfully this week must surely believe in inspiration—in guidance—in the power of God to direct our paths and to reveal to us His wisdom. This is one function of the quiet hour. When we become transparent and incandescent enough, when we abide in the poise of soul, and the peace of mind that passeth understanding, we shall not be surprised if the very heavens seem to open and we receive perfect guidance for our actions, divine inspiration for our words, and true revelation of God's eternal truth for ourselves and for others.

But while waiting for this high experience of inspiration and revelation, we must not be confused, or stopped by the mere *Stimulus* of a healthy appetite, and a passing emotion. We must not let a pressing sense of a personal *Need* blind us to the larger social *Need*. We must not let a personal *Desire*, uncorrelated with other and larger group needs, sway and control us. We must examine a *Hunch* to see whether it is a good or bad hunch. We can give serious consideration to a hunch only when it becomes a quiet and persistent *Urge*.

Not until we have completely given ourselves to our Father, not until we have mounted to the place of selflessness and love, and find the peace that passeth understanding, may we expect true divine *Guidance* to come to us, as well as true *Inspiration*, and true *Revelation*.

```
                                              REVELATION
                                      INSPIRATION
                            GUIDANCE
                     URGE
              HUNCH
         DESIRE
     NEED
STIMULUS
```

I have found that all great poets and true artists have a
feeling that the Great Song has been already sung—that
all they have to do is to tune in to the source of power
and let the great All-Song sing through them. Gutson
Borglum said, as you remember, that he did not do anything to the rock, he merely cut away the pieces—the
statue was already there.

You will attain the level of true inspiration and true
revelation much more quickly if you can believe that your
Divine Plan is already out ahead of you in God's scheme,
that your work is already done in this great universe—
that all you have to do is to tune in and trace the lines
that your Heavenly Father has already drawn for you.

Let us climb up the stairway of Inspiration from the
low levels where we do things for ourselves, to the higher
levels where God does things for us. What a blessed
privilege! And how wonderful our own work becomes
when we put our plan in complete accord with God's
great plan for us.

II. *Self-control*.—The one who trusts much to his urge
and his inspiration, should balance it with temperance
and self-control. The chief dangers for those who depend

upon inspiration alone are that they may become like weather vanes, pliant to every wind that blows, or else that they may become fanatical in driving through some narrow, rigid, set plan regardless of consequences. But the moment you bring to your quiet hour the spirit of a wide temperance, where humor and common sense balance your zeal and ardor, where a wide grasp of the whole picture prevents one-sided and narrow conclusions, then you are safe. The difference between a fanatic and a man of vision, is that the latter takes in all the picture, the former looks at only half; the latter looks at the great end, the former worships the little means; the latter sees it in relation to everything else; the former sees one road, and one road only.

I know of nothing more characteristic of the highest spiritual leadership than this balance of true inspiration and true self-control. Little leaders often have no desires, or if they have they are narrow-minded and perhaps fanatical desires. Great leaders have tremendous urges and desires, but they are held in such balance and control that they create good and never bad. Great men are broad-minded, sympathetic with the weak, compassionate with sinners, cooperative with enemies, loyal to friends.

But self-control is of value not only in balancing and checking up inspiration, but it is of value in balancing all other virtues and attributes of the Spirit, which we have been considering. Temperance and self-control enable one to be transparent, and yet filled with faith; meek, and at the same time have the certainty that makes one feel that one could remove mountains. Self-control makes it possible for one to love his friend to the point of adoration, and yet be able, if God wills, to relinquish that

friend to separation or death, finding in that relinquishment a peace that passeth all understanding.

                                          GOD-MASTERY
                                    SELF-MASTERY
                              POISE
                        BALANCE
                  SELF-CONTROL
            TEMPERANCE
      MODERATION
SELF-DENIAL

Self-control enables one who has attained to a perfection and goodness above his neighbors, to be humble
enough to forgive the sins, and compassionate enough to
be tolerant with the sinner. In this *Balance* we find a
doorway that leads us into heaven. It is self-control that
enables one who has gone through a long night of suffering or trial that would exhaust most men's fortitude and
patience, to come up in the morning with *Poise*, unsha-
ken because *Self-mastery* has given place to *God-mastery*.
So let us travel up the trail of *Temperance* and *Self-control*,
side by side with the trail of inspiration and revelation.
Pray today, not that God will destroy your dreams and
aspirations and ambitions, but that He will give you self-
control to relinquish them into His hands, and rest in
perfect peace in the plan that He has for you. Carry this
into every area of life, relinquishing every lower motive,
every lower purpose, every lower craving, to the greatest
purpose and highest motive that God has for us. Thus we
rise from the lowest steps of *Self-denial* and *Moderation*,
up to the highest step of *God-mastery*.

MEDITATION

Jesus, knowing that . . . He was come from God, and went to God, . . . began to wash the disciples' feet (John 13:3,5). (Read I Cor. 14:1-33.)

PRAYER

Our Father, anoint us with Thy Spirit, that we shall be truly inspired of Thee. Think through us, speak through us, act through us. But above all give us the gift of common sense and self-control that all things may be done to Thy glory and Thy honor from the greatest that we do unto the least. Amen.

SIXTH DAY

THE PRAYER OF POWER AND PRAISE

I. Power.—After five days of experiencing the power of prayer through the avenues and stairways that lead to the throne of God, it behooves us to sit down before this infinite, irresistible power, and contemplate it in all its wonderful aspects. Power is granted to man largely according to his understanding of it, and according to his wisdom in the use of it. How far can we understand it, and realize it, and experience it?

Our first acquaintance with power is in the form of force or effort. The little boy thinks that the brawny ditch-digger, throwing up huge spadefuls of earth, is a much more powerful figure than the neatly clad rather dapper young man manipulating levers in a protected room. He can hardly believe that each stroke of the lever in the hand of the apparently inactive man sets a giant traveling-crane in motion, which lifts, in each operation, more dirt than the brawny, perspiring ditch-digger can lift in a day. The contrast between these two working figures is our first and last lesson in power. It teaches us that, nine times out of ten, the smaller and the more invisible the effort, the greater the outflow of power. It teaches us that the more we depend upon forces that are greater than ourselves, through reverence and understanding and discipline, the more powerful our efforts shall become.

The shorter the wave length, the further the radio sounds will carry. The smaller the light beam, the farther the cosmic rays will penetrate. The smaller the germ, the more virulent the disease. But the greatest fact in all of this cluster of facts is that the more invisible your prayer, the more powerful it will become.

When we learn how to subdivide the atoms that are in a spoonful of water there will be enough power released from that one spoonful of water to carry an ocean liner from New York to Liverpool and back again.

When we have learned how to render our prayer invisible and humble and selfless enough, there will be enough power in one prayer to move mountains, to heal invalids, to save souls, to create poems, to end wars, and

---

                                        OMNIPOTENCE
                                  DOMINION
                            POWER
                      MIGHT
                 STRENGTH
            ENERGY
       EFFORT
FORCE

---

to bring the Kingdom of Heaven into manifestation upon earth.

It is very fitting for us to pause in awe in the presence of the marvelous scientific inventions of this age—the radio, the airplane, air-conditioning, television, and all of the myriad wonders of electricity, light, and sound. But do not let us neglect to pause in even greater awe before the mysterious forces in our inner soul. Now let us lift our gaze from the little *Force* and *Effort* and *Energy* that the ditch-digger exercises with such futility, up to the *Strength* and *Might* and *Power* of the more invisible forces of the Spirit. Let us not stop there, but reach up into the place of selflessness and oneness and peace, where the *Dominion* and *Omnipotence* of Almighty God can work through us, his mighty wonders to perform.

II. Praise.—Power should always be accompanied by praise. They are partners, if there ever were partners, in the realm of the Spirit. Your gratitude and praise should be in measure to the greatness of the power which you have witnessed. So, taking the ladder of *Praise*, climb to the topmost round, and there grant the glory and the Praise and the Adoration, to the One from whom all blessings flow. The accompanying ladder tells its own story. You are expert enough by this time to climb your own ladder without much help from me. Climb it joyously and thankfully, noting the great advance you make with each step.

The lowest form of gratitude is the sense of *Indebtedness* to another. This comes usually with a sense of weight, and it is resented more often than accepted. If accepted, it becomes a sense of *Obligation*, usually an unwilling obligation. When this is lifted to the place of open *Acknowledgment*, you are passing through the doorway to

ADORATION

PRAISE

THANKSGIVING

GRATITUDE

APPRECIATION

ACKNOWLEDGMENT

OBLIGATION

INDEBTEDNESS

---

a higher level, the first ledge of which opens on *Apprecia-tion*. Now self is dropping out, and God commences to enter in and before you know it you are rising through the successive stages of *Gratitude* and *Thanksgiving*, until you stand on the very summit of *Praise* and *Adoration*. There take up your abode and let your thanksgiving, praise and adoration rise like incense, night and day, to the Glory of God.

MEDITATION

He giveth power to the faint; and to them that have no might He increaseth strength. Even the youths shall faint and be weary, and the young men shall utterly fall: but they that wait upon the Lord shall renew their strength; they shall mount up with wings as eagles; they shall run, and not be weary; and they shall walk, and not faint (Isa. 40:29,30). Praise ye the Lord. Praise ye the Lord from the Heavens: praise Him in the heights (Ps. 148:1). Thus saith the Lord, let not the wise man glory in his wisdom, neither let the mighty man glory in his might, let not the rich man glory in his riches: but let him that glorieth glory in this, that he understandeth and knoweth Me, that I am the Lord which exercise lovingkindness, judgment, and righteousness, in the earth: for in these things I delight, saith the Lord (Jer. 9:23,24). (Read Ps. 145.)

PRAYER

Our Father, we know that with Thee, all things are possible. There is no power but from Thee. For Thine is the kingdom and the power and the glory forever and ever. Amen.

SEVENTH DAY
THE PRAYER ON THE MOUNTAIN TOP
Having made your feet like "hind's feet" and having climbed the twelve stairways of the Spirit, you have at last reached the highest mountain of prayer to which I can guide you. If you would go further you must seek another guide.

Taking our stand upon this high eminence, let us see if it would not be possible to so blend together all of the great attributes of the spirit that we could send forth a prayer that would bless the whole world.

During this week's meditations we have seen that by synchronizing two great virtues of the spirit each day, we could increase the power of our prayer. If the blending of two virtues can strengthen our prayer, just think how much more powerful our prayer might become if we could synchronize *all* of these twelve virtues of the spirit, for a continuous and eternal prayer! I believe that such a thing is possible. Let us prayerfully attempt to achieve this synchronization in this hour. On the next page you will find a diagram indicating the twelve stairways to the mountain top. On the summit are three "microphones of prayer" in the form of three circles, one within another.

The inner circle is the "microphone" which the aver-

age person uses. It is a very ineffective instrument. The
prayer which moves through this circle starts with *Belief*,
and moves through the lower levels of the spirit. The love
in it rarely rises above *Affection*, and it depends for its ef-
fectiveness upon the *Force* (mental and psychic) with
which it is directed upon the object prayed for. It ends
with a feeling of *Humiliation*, or of *Obligation*, or both,
and does not bring the sense of triumphant peace we are
seeking.

As a matter of fact this smaller circle of prayer does not
belong on the *top* of the mountain at all, but in reality
functions down at the mountain's foot, as indicated in
the diagram. I merely duplicated it above in order to
show it in relation to the other two circles of prayer.

The second circle, which, by the way, actually functions about two-thirds up the mountain-side, just about
one step above the level of John the Baptist's prayer, is
the prayer of the average Christian when he is at his very
highest inspiration. It was the highest level of prayer, by
the way, which I had attained when I wrote *The Soul's
Sincere Desire*.

I described it then in the form of a golf stroke, beginning with the drawing back of the golf club as far as it
will go, and ending with the perfect "follow through."
Such a prayer describes a complete circle—the most
beautiful, powerful, and permanent line that can be
drawn. In this circle of prayer we lift our consciousness as
far up toward God as we can in faith, then let it swing
down with love toward the one prayed for. The love in
turn creates joy, and the joy in turn creates the spirit of
power that achieves the miracle of fulfillment. This fulfillment, which takes its rise outside ourselves, gives rise
to a sense of humility, and inspires in us the sense of

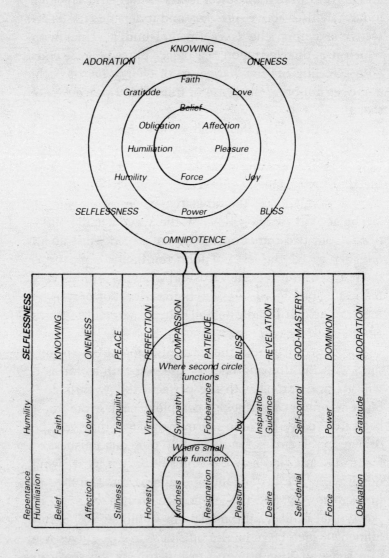

gratitude to the Infinite Power which has produced the miracle. This humility and gratitude, empty of self, let God enter and fill us, thus drawing our thought up again to God, where our prayer first began. And now we are ready to start the prayer all over again. Thus the round repeats itself. This is the finest example of perpetual motion of which I know.

But high as this form of prayer is, there is still a higher form. Let us turn now to the outer circle—the "microphone," which deserves the right to stand in this place of the most high. And as we send our prayers through it we find that we are using the most heavenly and most irresistible prayer that man is capable of praying.

This is the prayer that Jesus used. He gives a perfect model of it in His last great prayer when He dedicated His disciples to spread His gospel, and left His final blessing upon them.

First, as all who pray should do, He lifted up His eyes to God, "These words spake Jesus, and lifted up His eyes to Heaven, and said, Father, the hour is come; glorify Thy Son, that Thy Son may glorify Thee; as Thou hast given Him power over all flesh, that He should give eternal life to as many as Thou hast given Him."

Here He stands in the place of *Knowing*:

"And this is life eternal, that they might *know* Thee, the only true God, and Jesus Christ whom Thou hast sent.

"I have glorified Thee on the earth; I have finished the work which Thou gavest me to do. And now, O Father, glorify Thou me with Thine own self, with the glory which I had with Thee before the world was. I have manifested Thy name unto the men which Thou gavest me out of the world: Thine they were, and Thou gavest them me; and they have kept Thy word.

"Now they have *known* that all things whatsoever Thou hast given me are of Thee.

"For I have given unto them the words which Thou gavest me; and they have received them, and have *known* surely that I came out from Thee, and they have believed that Thou didst send Me."

Note how the word *know* and *known* are repeated three times above.

Now He steps onward into the place of *Oneness*:

"I pray for them: I pray not for the world, but for them which Thou hast given Me; for they are Thine. And all Mine are Thine, and Thine are Mine: and I am glorified in them. And now I am no more in the world, but these are in the world, and I came to Thee. Holy Father, keep through Thine own name those whom Thou hast given Me, that they may be *One*, even as We are."

Next He steps into *Joy*:

"And now I come to Thee; and these things I speak in the world, that they might have My *Joy* fulfilled in themselves."

Finally He gives His specific prayer for His disciples, letting the *Omnipotence* of God move through it. This prayer is twofold—for protection for His followers from evil, and for the consecration of them in the service of God.

"I pray not that Thou shouldst take them out of the world, but that Thou shouldst keep them from the evil. They are not of the world, even as I am not of the world. Sanctify them through Thy truth: Thy word is truth. As Thou hast sent Me into the world, even so I also sent them into the world. And for their sakes I sanctify Myself, that they also might be sanctified through the truth."

Next He prays another prayer, a prayer within a prayer, and this time His prayer is for us, for you and for me, and for all of those who "believe through their word." Note how His prayer for us is primarily centered upon our achieving this oneness with each other and with Him—a blessing which Jesus evidently valued above all other blessings. This is emphasized by His repeating the word *one* five times.

"Neither pray I for these alone, but for them also which shall believe on Me through their word; that they may all be *one*; even as Thou, Father, art in Me, and I in Thee, that they also may be *one* in Us: that the world may believe that Thou hast sent Me. And the glory which Thou gavest Me I have given them; that they may be *one*, even as We are *one*; I in them and Thou in Me, that they may be made perfect into *one*; and that the world may know that Thou hast sent Me, and hast loved them, even as Thou hast loved Me."

Out of this *Oneness* will come *Omnipotence, Transparency, Adoration*, and all the rest of the virtues in our ladder of heaven.

"Father, I will that they also, Thou hast given Me, be with Me where I am; that they may behold My glory, which Thou hast given Me: for Thou lovest Me before the foundation of the world. O righteous Father, the world hath not known Thee: but I have known Thee, and these have known that Thou hast sent Me. And I have declared unto them Thy Name, and will declare it: that the love wherewith Thou hast loved Me may be in them, and I in them."

Using this prayer as a model, let us first lift our faith in God to the highest consciousness of absolute *knowing* that *He* is our strength and shield, then let us swing gently into the realization of our complete *oneness* with the one prayed for. Let us rest in this consciousness until the realization of *bliss* comes. That realization is the signal that God's Omnipotent *power* is released for our need, and that our prayer is answered in heaven. Then let us turn to the "follow through" part of the prayer, letting our little selves fade out of the picture in absolute *selflessness, transparency* and *incandescence*, as we give to the Father all the *praise* and the *glory*. This selflessness and adoration immediately let God in, and we are ready to start the perfect round of prayer all over again.

While only six of the twelve stairways are represented in this circle, the other six are there in essence. The Peace that passeth understanding could be used instead of Bliss, Compassion instead of Love, Patience instead of Selflessness, and Revelation or Perfection instead of Omnipotence. I am merely trying to show you how, if there is power in blending two virtues, there is even greater power in blending six or twelve. Thus one's prayer can become a solo, a duet, or even a chorus, as it moves from a slender melody of one note of our inner being, to a harmony of all the notes of our inner being.

In conclusion let me say that when you step into this holy of holies, you do not really do the praying any more. The Holy Spirit does the praying for you. When you *know* that God is completely adequate for your needs, it is God's mind knowing it through you. When you love a person to the height of oneness, it is not your little heart doing the loving, it is really the great cosmic love of the Infinite God flowing through you. The bliss that suffuses you is not something that your tiny veins and arteries create in you, it is a gift of God from the very heaven of heavens. And certainly the Omnipotent Power which creates the miracle is none of your creating—it comes entirely from the Holy Spirit working through you.

Now that you have attained to this high eminence of Spirit, you stand upon holy ground. Take the shoes from off your feet, bow your head in humble adoration of the Most High. Then give the great needs of yourself and others entirely to the Father of Infinite Love, letting this great broadcasting station of the Holy Spirit wing them forth to the place where all of our prayers are answered.

MEDITATION

I know, that even now, whatsoever thou wilt ask of God, God will give it thee (John 11:22). Put on, therefore, as God's elect, holy and beloved, a heart of compassion, kindness, humility, meekness, long-suffering; forbearing one another, and forgiving each other if any man have a complaint against any; even as the Lord forgave you, also do ye: and above all these things put on love which is the bond of perfectness (Col. 3.12,13). And whatsoever ye shall ask in My name, that will I do, that the Father may be glorified in the Son. If ye shall ask anything in My name, I will do it (John 14:13,14). (Read John 15:1-16.)

PRAYER

Our Father, we thank Thee that Thou hast made us Thy sons and not Thy hirelings, that Thou hast made us heirs and co-heirs with Christ. Pray through us, dream through us, vision through us, so that our prayers may be of the warp and woof of eternity—coming from eternity and going on into eternity—infinite and irresistible, bringing blessings to all mankind. Amen.

IV

Gifts That Are Yours

Until I made the first discovery of "hind's feet," life was full of difficulties and perplexities for me. I was not satisfied with my work, not satisfied with my town, not satisfied with my health, not satisfied with the way Fate was dealing with me. Not that I was giving way to self-pity! If there was any deep conviction intrenched in my soul it was that the greatest of sinners are those who pity themselves. Nor was I cynical and misanthropic toward others. I simply knew that there was something wrong with myself. I held fast to my ideals of sweetness and goodness, but, like a clock running down, my whole system of goodness and sweetness was growing less and less effective, until the heart within me was hardly beating at all. The salt of my life had truly lost its savor. The lamp of my faith was fast becoming smothered under a bushel. Life was all gray.

And then, almost overnight, everything changed. If this world was so dull, and empty and unexciting, I said to myself, why not make one's feet into "hind's feet" and step into another world? And so, just as simply as Alice stepped through the looking-glass, I stepped into the Kingdom of Heaven.

The path I took I have been trying to describe to you in this book. As a matter of fact, it was so simple that it could easily be described as merely getting up in the morning on the other side of bed. I simply shifted all my thinking from the wrong side over to the right side of my heart and brain. In other words, I merely surrendered my heart and will and mind—both conscious and subconscious—to the Great Superconscious Mind of God.

A new joy and a new radiance now lighted me. Something about this radiance shining outwardly drew to me new friends. Something about this radiance shining inwardly drew to me new ideas. The new friends and the new ideas were marvelously happy together. The two together combined to create for me a veritable Kingdom of God on earth. Everything about me moved in beautiful accord. And yet how hard it was to explain to others what and how my life had changed!

I was coaching the track team of my college and was told I would have to limit our traveling expenses for the season to two hundred dollars, whereas our rival colleges had ten times that amount. Instead of approaching the task with a long face and a heavy heart, as I had done in preceding seasons, I joyously accepted the challenge and asked the Father to take over the burden. The way opened for me to take the team on as many long trips as the other colleges, securing amazing rates for some trips, and actual rebates on others. Four long trips that would ordinarily cost as much as two thousand dollars, cost me only one hundred and ninety dollars. Other years followed with still greater manifestations of God's guidance and care.

One of my track boys caught the thing that had taken hold of me. It began to radiate so from his face that students told me that his smile, as he went by them in the morning, made their whole day go better.

I was called to the University of Wisconsin and talked to the track team about this lad. I talked on spiritual adjustment, not on winning contests; on getting in tune with God, not on getting the best of one's opponents. A handsome boy, slightly bowlegged, came to me and grasped my hand and said, "I want to get that." Two weeks later the Big Ten Indoor Field Meet was to be held. The morning paper said, "The championship lies between Illinois, Iowa, and Ohio." The next day the paper said, "The surprise of the meet was the way Wisconsin ran away with the meet, led by a little bowlegged chap they couldn't stop."

In all these things I asked nothing. I merely gave the situation wholly and completely to God. I merely shared with others in creating attitudes of harmony and trust. *Then God worked the miracle!*

Perhaps the most startling experiences in my new life of living in the Kingdom were the little excursions from time to time, when the need called, that I was enabled to take into the undimensional realm of Eternity, while still sojourning in the realm of Time. Then it was that for brief moments even the prophet's mantle fell upon me.

One night, as I was locking my car in the garage I rented from my neighbor, the fierce bulldog kept to guard the place leaped at me the full length of his chain as he had done every time I came near him. Just as I was preparing to put the padlock on the door that night, an inner voice seemed to tell me—so clear came the realization—that the *next moment the dog would break his chain*. For months the dog had been fastened there and never had the chain broken. But, trusting this guidance, I withdrew the padlock, stepped inside the garage, and drew the door shut after me. The same instant the chain broke and the full weight of the dog crashed against the door.

Later in the same year, two students asked me why I was so sure that we were not to have a war with Japan. I turned to God for guidance and suddenly heard myself saying, "Because Japan as a military nation will be destroyed by an earthquake." "How soon?" they asked, and immediately I heard myself saying, "Within the next six months."

Five months after that date the earthquake occurred that reduced Japan from a first-class to a third-class fighting nation overnight, destroyed its shipping-yards and its treasury and about one hundred thousand lives.

Why could Japan not have prayed away the earthquake, as I saved myself from the dog? I believe sincerely that had the entire Japanese nation turned to God in prayer, the earthquake could have been averted. I believe that bad events out there in Time, like bridges that go down out there in Space, are not something we have to run into "head on." I believe that when we foresee collisions in Time, just as when we foresee collisions in Space, we can make safe detours around them. I believe that that is the reason that God sends us prophetic insight at times. Why should He otherwise ever need to forewarn us?

Of late years I have witnessed marvelous answers to group prayers, where two or three, or even seventy, have come together agreeing in Jesus' name on what they should ask for. Some of these prayers have been for individual needs, but more often for national or international matters, proving that Sherwood Eddy was right when he said, "If I could find twelve men *completely* surrendered to God, I could change the aspect of America."

I profoundly believe that if seventy people, who actually and positively and unswervingly believe in the power of prayer, would come together, they could solve all the problems of America.

I have found, nevertheless, that there are strange limitations placed upon my prayers, limitations, however, which are man made, not God made. For instance, I find it very hard to pray for one who does not seek my prayers, and almost impossible to pray for one who absolutely disbelieves in prayer. I find it impossible to pray for financial supply for a man who disregards or refuses to pay his honest debts. It is hard to pray *with* anyone, or *for* anyone who hates another. And it is next to impossible to pray for anyone who is so filled with fear or care that he has no room left for "silent spaces" in his being. Oh, that we had more time in this busy world to build more silent spaces into our souls!

There is only one prayer that I pray regularly every morning of my life—and that is that I may abide in the Kingdom of Heaven every moment of the day, and inspire others to abide there also. This is the prayer that encompasses and completes all other prayers. It is the prayer which, when prayed with understanding faith, never fails of fulfillment.

There are two ways into the Kingdom of Heaven. One we may call the way of life, and one we may call the way of death. Just because one of these ways seems to us, who are living on this earth plane, as the happier way, is no conclusive proof that those who are taken by the will of God through the valley and the shadow of death have not found a still more radiant way. Let us change a motto which all real Christians abhor because it reeks of materialism and selfishness: "Our country! May she always be right; but *our* country, right or wrong!" into a motto that thrills with selflessness and celestial light: "*Thy* kingdom first, either here or there, but always *Thy* kingdom." If the only way to attain that kingdom is by the road of death, I would gladly give myself, my dearest friends, yes, even my own children, if it were the will of God, through the doorway of death into that happy country. But fortunately there is another way. And that way that sounds so hopelessly simple that it draws the smile of the cynic and the sneer of the materialist, is merely this: Become as a little child.

The little child is the one person who always walks with "hind's feet." To him, the conscious, the subconscious, and the superconscious are all one. "Whosoever shall not receive the Kingdom of God as a little child shall in no wise enter therein."

How I have pounded and hammered away at myself trying to melt the hardened metal of my own middle-aged heart into the softness and pliancy of a little child! How I have argued and expounded and exhorted my friends to turn and become as little children, and, how often, alack, to no avail! The only way I have consistently succeeded is when I have caught myself or others unawares, seated around a camp fire, or looking into the restful waters of a lake or ocean, and spontaneously and casually related a fairy story. A fairy story is like a painless surgical operation. It furnishes, in the first place, an anaesthetic that puts the outer cynical, always guarding and always menacing Logic and Worldly Wisdom, to sleep. Next it opens hidden passages, lost since the days of youth, that lead back to childhood attitudes and aptitudes, to old enthusiasms and long-forgotten memories, passageways that lead back to the springtime freshness of life and enable the old poison sacs of cynicism and materialism to drain off before anyone knows what is happening. Then, starting with brand-new clean flesh, even as of a little child, the stricken soul is allowed to start anew. Yes, unless you turn and become as a little

child there is no need for me to talk further with you
about entering into the Kingdom of Heaven. So, ere we
bring our little journey to a close, draw your chair up to
the fireplace and let me tell you a fairy tale.

Once upon a time there was a boy named Jack, who
was the son of an old lady who had been married to a
king. A giant had killed the king and banished the queen
and her little boy. And now, as an old lady, the queen
was working hard to keep the bodies and souls of herself
and her son together, with only a cow and a patch of land
to assist her.

At last all of her money was gone, and she was forced
to send her boy to town to exchange the cow for money
that would keep mother and son in food a little longer.
On the way to town Jack met a man with a sheep, who
persuaded him that a sheep was more valuable than a
cow. Then came a man with a pig, and this man had an
equally persuasive tongue. Then Jack accepted a goose,
next a hen, and finally he returned to his mother with
only a handful of beans to show for all of his bargaining.

I don't think any of us would blame the mother for losing her temper and throwing the beans out of the window. I think we would have done exactly the same thing.
But she was little prepared for what followed. After what
I hope was a sound night's sleep, she awoke the next
morning to behold a great network of beanstalks growing
up beside the house. Jack immediately saw an opportunity no boy could miss and he climbed a beanstalk. At the
top of it he found a great tableland, a sort of island in the
air. This proved to be the home of a giant and his wife,
the same giant who had dispossessed his mother and
himself and killed his father. The giant (he of the famous

lines, "fee, fi, fo, fum, I smell the blood of an English-man") would have destroyed him had he caught him, but the giantess was glad to help him, knowing as she did that these possessions were the boy's by right, and in her heart (God bless her!) she had always hoped that some day the rightful owner would come and claim them. Jack made three journeys to this giant's stronghold, and each time brought back one of the precious treasures that the giant had stolen from his father. One was a little red hen which would lay a golden egg each day; another was a harp which, without human aid, would play beautiful music; and the last was a magic carpet that would convey one wherever he wished to go.

Now, to me this is not a fairy tale, but one of the most real of all the documents of human life. We are all sons of a King. All of our lives we are trading beans for cattle, or cattle for beans. Some of us never do anything else. We all have the opportunity some time or other to climb beanstalks. And some of us have experienced the thrill of knowing what it means to have the little red hen that lays the golden egg whenever we need it, to have the harp that sends the right ideas singing through our minds at the right time, and to find ourselves in the place we wish to be, at the very moment we wish to be there, and with the very people we wish to have with us! Have you ever found a more perfect description of the Kingdom of Heaven manifesting itself on earth than that? And to think that all of this may be obtained by merely turning and becoming as a little child!

How I should love to pass this secret on to others in such a way that they could actually see it, could actually believe it, and above all could actually experience it! But only those who have gathered around the fireplace with the open hearts of little children can have any chance of grasping a secret as deep as this. Of course a great deal more is involved in the attitude of mind of becoming like a little child than most people dream. It not only involves the matter of "believing," but also the matter of "seeing," or of inner interpreting. The true child is not only a dreamer, but he is also a seer. *And the true seer looks through the outer crust to the inner heart of things.* Let us look through the outer shell into the inner meaning of the story of "Jack and the Beanstalk."

The first step that Jack took was to exchange the outer material things, the whole personal outer self, for the inner intangible things of the spirit. One gladly exchanges money for a college education, even the most hard headed among us have done that, but that exchange, alas, is too often made merely upon the condition of exchanging the college education back again for still more money—a sort of Indian gift, as it were. Few of us are willing to exchange the outer material things for those more intangible things such as love, peace, faith, temperance, and patience. We are more hesitant about exchanging our active boisterous busy times for periods of stillness, of silence, of quietness, and of prayer. We are glad to exchange our visions for stocks and bonds; too rarely are we willing to exchange gold and silver for visions.

The first thing that all true sons of Kings must know is that the smaller and more invisible a thing is, the more powerful and creative and precious it is. The first step which a son of a king must be ready to take is to exchange his outer bodily, selfish self for a brand-new, invisible, reborn inner self—to trade with perfect audacity the husks of an old, outworn mortality for a handful of seeds of a new, inner immortality.

Having gotten the seeds, the next thing is to throw them out of the window. If the soil they fall into has been cultivated in the past, all the better. If the soil in our heart is hungry for the seed, the situation is perfect. The next step for the son of a king is to go to sleep and forget what he has done. In the morning when he awakes he will make the great discovery that the seed, so seemingly insignificant, has built for him the ladder up to the island of his superconscious soul.

Then comes the difficult task of climbing up to this Kingdom of Heaven that is within him. This is where the need for "hind's feet" comes. In other words, this climbing can be made perfectly only when the climber trusts absolutely—with his subconscious mind as well as his conscious mind—in the strength of the vine that has grown from such tiny seeds as love, patience, gentleness, goodness, faith, meekness and temperance. These are the fruits of the spirit. . . . "Against such there is no law." If he cannot trust himself *completely* to the strength that lies in such delicate vines of the spirit, he will find it very difficult to climb to the Kingdom. Yes, it is easier for a camel to go through the eye of a needle than for one who trusts in outer riches to enter into the Kingdom of Heaven.

And now we have reached the place where we must leave the fairy story behind us. Only the greatest teachings in the Holy Scriptures will be adequate to carry us up the final ascent to the Kingdom. For there is one place where the legends and fairy stories of ancient bards fail us. It is at this point where we must turn to the parables and visions of Jesus. The fairy story lifts one to the subconscious plane, Jesus' vision lifts us to the superconscious realm. Jack merely lifts us to the edge of the wilderness. Like John the Baptist, he can take us no farther than the great "no man's land" of the psychic forces of good and evil, those great pairs of opposites—one of which is aligned with good—sympathetic and helpful; the other is aligned with evil—bitterly arrayed against us, ready to destroy us at any false step.

That part of our subconsciousness that would oppose us is the spirit of cynicism and materialism and worldly reason that has grown in our race mind until it has become a veritable giant. This giant lives entirely upon the premise that the larger and more visible a thing is the more powerful it is; it denies all power and reality to anything that cannot be seen, like love, faith, peace, and goodness. But, fortunately, there has also been growing up in the racial mind during all the centuries another and "better half" to this subconscious giant—a feminine, intuitional, trusting, believing spirit which will come to our aid if we accept it, and which will protect us and guide us into the heritage that every true son of the King has a right to possess.

And so Jack returns with the threefold gift—the power of receiving money when he needs it, of receiving ideas when he needs them, and of being in the place where he wishes to be when he needs to be there.

Jesus has interpreted for us the message of this story in his parables of the "Pearl without Price" and the "Mustard Seed." First we see a man exchanging cattle, pigs, sheep, anything and everything he owns, for one little pearl. If we should go one step further and convert this precious stone into a grain of wheat, we would carry this process to its logical conclusion. For we could then render the pearl, which is *almost* invisible because it is so small, completely invisible by placing it in the ground. "Except a grain of wheat fall into the ground and die, it abideth alone: but if it die, it bringeth forth much fruit." Jesus tells the parable of the mustard seed to show how the smallest of seeds, when rendered completely invisible by being buried in the earth, grows to be a great tree, and birds come and nest in the branches thereof. These birds bring the little hen that lays the golden egg, the harp that sings, and the carpet that travels. Is not all this implied in "Ask, and it shall be given you; seek, and ye shall find; knock, and it shall be opened unto you"?

I do not say that trusting completely and utterly in God will make us all giants in strength or absolutely perfect in health or Adonises in beauty. But I do believe that it will help to create health in us—yes, strength and beauty—as nothing else can. I do not say that trusting in God will make us rich as Crœsus, but I do believe that it will open the door as nothing else can for the right amount to come to us at the right time to meet our actual needs. So utterly do I believe in this that when I have tried the best I can to save up for a thing that I thought I needed, and the money does not come, I accept it as definite guidance that it is best, in God's plan, for me not to have it. Nor do I say that trusting in God will make us all geniuses, and all models of wisdom, but I do believe with all the power of my being, and it has been borne out time after time in my own experience, that if we trust God completely enough, He will send us exactly the right ideas at exactly the right time. Thus far, I have found in my own experience, that God brings fulfillment in our lives similar to the fulfillment that came to Jack in the three gifts given to him by the giantess on the mountain top.

The only way to test out the validity of this beanstalk story is to step forth and actually try it. Fortunately, it is the easiest of all things to try. We all—no matter how poor we are—have the materials and capital right at hand to try it. A mere patch of ground and an old cow was enough for Jack to make his start. Merely to have an old body and an old mind, in short, an *old self*, is enough for any of us to make a very creditable start. Go down the road looking for Jesus. As soon as you find Him and He offers to trade you a New Self, take Him at His word and do it immediately. Do not haggle and do not bargain with Him. Surrender to His invitation instantly. At first it may appear as though you were losing in every trade. For the old self you give away will be a fairly matured, fairly wise, fairly experienced old fellow. He will know lots more than many folks, and he will be mighty proud of all that he knows. He may have old family prides that have been handed down to him from past generations. He may have vanities that are precious, hates and envies enough to fill a dray wagon; ambitions and jealousies enough to stock a department store. It is a tremendous lot you have to give away, and what will you get in exchange? Nothing to start with, perhaps, except a little Child lying in a manger. But do not despair. Wait until the tiny Child grows to complete Christhood and takes complete control of all your life, and then see what blessed things begin to happen to yourself and to others about you! Wonderful will be the blessings to you and to yours if you have the patience and courage to wait upon the Christ within you.

So take yourself to the market-place, along with Jack and his cow, and be prepared to exchange your big tangible values, like wealth and pride and position in life, for those small intangible fruits of the spirit, even more invisible than the beans that Jack received. But like the beans, they will grow stalks that will reach to the very heaven of heavens.

To make graphic what we have done, I have arranged in the preceding chapter the twelve "beanstalks" that have grown from the seeds of righteousness, and which flower above in the fruits of the spirit, all on one page. Let us assume that you have climbed to the summit of these vines, up into the "promised land" of the spiritual realm, the realm where all our prayers are answered. This realm is above the land which Jack of the Beanstalk found. His beanstalks carried him only up to the fifth or sixth "floor"—the realm where John the Baptist lived and moved and had his being—the realm where strong men take the Kingdom of Heaven by force. Let us journey past this realm of the "fee, fi, fo, fum" giants, up to the Kingdom of Heaven where abides the loving and merciful Father.

Having attained to this high realm, let us use our circle of prayer, like a colossal broadcasting station, and, like an expert broadcaster, let us feel our way to the outer rim, disdaining to use the little inner rim which is meant only for children and beginners, and there broadcast our prayers for this Kingdom to manifest itself in our lives upon this earth. First let us ask for the gift of Christ; second, let us ask for the gift of friends; third, let us ask for the gift of ideas; fourth, let us ask for the gift of the supply for our needs; fifth, let us ask for the gift of health; sixth, let us ask for the gift of guidance; and seventh, let us ask for the gift of world peace.

FIRST DAY

THE FATHER WILL GIVE YOU THE CHRIST

What is the test of true discipleship to Christ? Jesus gave it to us very simply in the closing hours in the Upper Room. "A new commandment I give unto you, that ye love one another; as I have loved you that ye also love one another. By this shall all men know that ye are My disciples, if ye have love one to another."

Love, then, is the test of discipleship. But there are different ways of loving. The "hireling" who prefers to abide in the jungle of materialism rather than in the Father's House where Christ has prepared a place for him, does not love in the way that Christ of the Upper Room loved us. The love of the hireling is not a heavenly love, but a jungle love which expresses itself in lust, greed, gluttony, ambition, passion, and possessiveness. The love of Christ's disciples is always distinguished from the jungle love by four qualities.

First, it does not stop with the outside of the person it loves. It penetrates to the heart and soul, and loves the inner spirit of him. If we love Christ, we will love the Father who sent Him.

Second, it loves the whole of the friend, and does not stop with merely a part—and that perhaps the easiest and most comfortable part. It has compassion for his shortcomings as well as joy in his strength. "He that hath my commandments (the hard as well as the easy ones), and keepeth them, he it is that loveth Me; and he that loveth Me shall be loved of My Father, and I will love him, and will manifest Myself to him."

Third, it is a love which is so strong and so real that it is willing to pay the price in discipline, in self-sacrifice, and in expenditure of time and energy to deserve his friendship. "Greater love hath no man than this, that a man lay down his life for his friends."

Fourth, it is a love which is so unselfish that it is willing to give away even that one whom it loves, if by doing so it will be possible for that one to come into more perfect realization of his perfect happiness, or into more perfect fulfillment of his life plan. "Ye have heard how I said unto you, I go away, and come again unto you. If ye loved me, ye would rejoice, because I said, I go unto the Father: for my Father is greater than I."

If you really want the Christ, and really and truly love Him, there is nothing that will prevent His coming and taking up His abode with you, provided your love for Him manifests itself in these four heavenly ways.

First, do you love the inner spirit of the Christ? This spirit, as you know, is the spirit of faith, the spirit of love, the spirit of compassion, the spirit of forgiveness, the spirit which says to the world "Come unto Me, all ye that labor and are heavy laden, and I will give you rest." Or do you merely want the *outside* of the Christ? Does your love stop with a beautiful *picture* of the Christ, a man with a flowing garment, long wavy hair, beautiful beard, and handsome eyes? If Christ should come today He would wear conventional clothes like all men wear, He would probably be without the familiar beard and would look like other men of today. Are you sure you would not reject Him as the Jews did before you, who were themselves eagerly awaiting the Messiah clothed in robes like Moses, and in trappings of outer authority like Solomon?

Do you love only a Jesus whose words are clothed in some certain man-made creed or doctrine? Will you accept only a Jesus who comes as a Baptist, or as an Anglican, or as a Lutheran? If you do you will certainly miss

Him if He should come again in human form. For Jesus came preaching no theology but a life, no doctrine but that of love. Think of thousands of people who cry, "Lord, Lord," who fail to see Christ because they refuse to look for the inner spirit and are prepared to accept Him only if He comes in a certain outer form, either of dress or of theological belief, or of churchly pattern. Jesus Himself tells how those will miss Him in the final day.

Do you love merely a picture of Jesus? Do you love only a historical Jesus? Or do you look through to the inner Christ—the Son of the Living God—expressing the Father in every thought, every word, and every act? If you see this inner Christ, He will come to you and abide with you forever.

Second, do you love all of Christ?

Many of us love the Christ of the church window and of the church altar, and of the chancel and the pew. How many of us love the Christ who said "Sell that thou hast and give to the poor?" How many of us love the Christ who ate and drank with sinners? How many of us love the Christ who spent more time in healing the sick than He did in preaching the gospel?

If we give thousands of dollars toward foreign missions and yet tolerate the child labor and sweatshop conditions in our own back yard, we are not seeing all of Jesus. If we think it foolish, fantastic, and unorthodox to depend upon prayer in time of illness, we are not seeing all of Jesus. Are we afraid that we shall be made an outcast if we who live in Atlanta work among Negroes; or if we who live in New York associate with the Jews; or if we who live in Los Angeles, cooperate with the Japanese? Are we afraid that we shall be branded as unclean if we show our love for harlots and publicans, for saloon-keep-

ers and gunmen? So branded they Jesus. Are we ortho-
dox Christians afraid that our friends will call us fanatical
if we pray with power for the sick? Are we afraid that
they will call us "Red" if we plead with earnestness for
social justice? Are we afraid that they will call us "im-
moral" if we work with tenderness and love among sinners, the unfortunate, and the fallen? If these fears deter
us, we do not love all of Christ.

Third, are we willing to pay the price for Christ?

Christ Himself was sold for thirty pieces of silver,
which was the exact sum set down in Deuteronomy for
the price of a man slave. To purchase Christ are you willing to give yourself into slavery for all eternity to Him?
Saul of Tarsus was willing to pay that price and he glor-
ied in that slavery. Are you willing to pay the price of forgiving all your enemies? Christ will certainly demand
that that price be paid to the last farthing before He will
give himself to you. Are you willing to tithe your wealth
if necessary? Christ may not demand that of you, but He
does of some. And many, many times He demands more.
He may require the cutting out of some dearly loved habit that is taking too great a toll from your deepest self. He
may require you to break off some fellowships with jolly
fellows, that do no good and only waste your time. He
may involve you in misunderstandings with old friends,
or bring upon you the slurs and sneers of your associates,
at least for a season. But in time all true love will win
back all true friends and make them truer than ever.

But the first price you will have to pay if you would
receive the Christ, the first sacrifice required of all of us,
is this: Are you willing to set aside a quiet hour each
morning, for at least three months? Are you willing to
keep that tryst with Him? If you are, you have made the

first step toward paying the price for attaining the blessed fellowship of the Christ. And it will not be the last. But let me tell you that there is nothing more glorious, more joyous, more rewarding than the faithful, unremitting, daily, yearly payments that you shall be asked to make in the years that are ahead, for so great a reward as the blessed Jesus.

Fourth, are you willing to give Jesus to others?

Are you willing to pass Jesus on to others in every way that you can? One way of passing Jesus on to others is in open testimony and sharing. A still better way is in living Jesus in your daily life so completely that He radiates out from your very spirit. The best way is not in *talking about* Him, but in *living* Him in your daily life. The second best way is in spoken testimony regarding the new and important place He now plays in your life. But the most difficult way of all, because it requires so great humility and tolerance and selflessness, is to be willing to behold others testifying for Jesus in ways different from our way, and doing it with so great power and devotion and sincerity, that it makes our little testimony seem infinitely small beside it.

Here is where the true test of our worthiness to possess Jesus is revealed. For it is so hard to prevent our own little jealousy, our own little sense of criticism, our own little intolerance, narrowness, and envy from seeking the first place among the witnesses. It is so easy, oh, so easy—to rise in righteous indignation and denounce others as "anti-Christs," as unorthodox, as hypocrites, as interlopers, as fanatics, as extremists, etc. It is so easy for the fundamentalists to deny the modernists any right to follow Christ in their way. It is so easy for the millennialists to call the social reformers pagans, and for the radicals to

call the conservatists hypocrites. ANY SECT OR GROUP
THAT PRETENDS TO BE CHRISTIAN AND FIGHTS ANOTHER
GROUP THAT BELIEVES IN CHRIST, AND WASTES PRECIOUS
TIME THAT COULD WELL BE SPENT IN UNITED ATTACK UPON
THE DEVIL, IN CRIMINATION AND RECRIMINATION, DOES NOT
DESERVE TO HAVE THE CHRIST.

But, when you love Christ in this fourfold way: love
His inner spirit, love all of Him, and are willing to pay
the price for Him, and, finally, are willing to give Him
away to any other person or group of persons who can
more vitally spread His cause than you can do—then THE
CHRIST WILL COME TO YOU AND ENTER INTO YOUR HEART
AND BLESS YOU THROUGH ALL ETERNITY.

MEDITATION

Come unto Me, all ye that labor and are heavy laden,
and I will give you rest. Take My yoke upon you and
learn of Me; for I am meek and lowly in heart; and ye
shall find rest unto your souls. For My yoke is easy and
My burden is light (Matt. 11:28-30). I am persuaded, that
neither death, nor life, nor angels, nor principalities, nor
powers, nor things present, nor things to come, nor
height, nor depth, nor any other creature, shall be able to
separate us from the love of God, which is in Christ Jesus
our Lord (Rom. 8:38,39). (Read Col. 3:1-17.)

PRAYER

Our Father, we ask not for the world and its pomp and glo-
ry, we merely ask for Thee. In Thyself alone is satisfaction
and abundance for our hearts. Thou hast created these hearts
for Thyself. Take out of them anything that is opposed to
Thee and enter and fill them. For our hearts cannot find rest
in aught but Thee. Amen.

SECOND DAY

THE FATHER WILL GIVE YOU FRIENDS

What you love loves you. Love is the great magnet, the greatest of all drawing-powers. If you love people, people will love you. If you love them in the fourfold heavenly way we considered yesterday, nothing can prevent their being drawn to you.

First, do you love the spirit of your friend, or do you just love the outside of him? If you love his clear complexion, his baritone voice, his straight Greek profile, his splendid figure, and stop there—then your love is not the true penetrating heavenly love. But if you love the deep wells of quietness, deep, deep down inside of him, if you love the Christlike quality of his compassion, or his yet unawakened capacity for intelligence, for endurance, for heroism, then you are beginning to get to the roots of him. Each person has a slightly different quality of personality, a different soul through which he expresses the great God Spirit. If you penetrate to that inner soul and love it—not some imaginary illusion or some imaginary pattern that you yourself place on him from without, but *his own true soul*, and love it—then he is really and truly your friend. You and he will be David and Jonathan for life, or Ruth and Naomi, as the case may be.

Second, do you love all of him? Many marriages fail because a girl falls in love with and marries a handsome face and a charming dancer, and awakens later to find that she has married an absent-minded scholar, or a cold-blooded business man, or a self-centered fisherman. Find out all of your friend, all sides of him, and if you are willing to accept all of him—his joking proclivity, his religious bent, his teasing moments, his serious hours—if you really and truly love the allness of him and the wholeness of him, then he truly belongs to you.

Third, are you willing to pay the price? The price of friendship is the act of being a true friend yourself. If you are a wallflower, unsought, undesired, start loving the other "wall-flowers" around you—the loveless and lonely and the forlorn, right about you. This act is what might be called "priming the well." As you give out to people the kind of love which they need from others, the love which you need will come to *you*.

Fourth, are you willing to give the friends that are drawn to you away? In other words, do you want them for your own personal satisfaction, for your own personal convenience, for your own comfort and pleasure and use? If you do they will tire of you, they will become satiated with you, and will turn away and depart, leaving you alone. As you give these great and glorious friends of yours away to serve and help others, you will suddenly find that they are doing your work for you, they are multiplying you, they are helping folks that you yourself cannot and could not help. And, above all, you will find the more you send them away with your joyous acceptance and kindly blessing upon them, the more they will come back to you and hold fast to you, in a comradeship of the spirit that will last through all eternity.

If you really love your friends in all these four ways, in other words, if you love them with all your heart and mind and soul and strength, then you have a right to pray that God will give you friends. Stand as high as you can on the Mountain of Prayer, open as wide as you can the Microphone of Communion with the Father, and as simply and as trustingly as a little child ask your Heavenly Father to send you the friends that He has prepared for you from the beginning of time, and your prayer will be answered in God's perfect way.

MEDITATION

And Jonathan said unto David, Come, and let us go out into the field. And they went out both of them into the field. And Jonathan caused David to swear again, because he loved him: for he loved him as he loved his own soul. And Jonathan said to David, Go in peace, forasmuch as we have sworn both of us in the name of the Lord, saying, the Lord be between me and thee, and between my seed and thy seed forever. And he arose and departed: and Jonathan went into the city (I Sam. 20:11,17,42). And Ruth said, Entreat me not to leave thee, or to return from following after thee: for whither thou goest, I will go; and where thou lodgest, I will lodge; thy people shall be my people, and thy God my God. So Naomi returned, and Ruth the Moabitess, her daughter-in-law, with her, which returned out of the country of Moab: and they came to Bethlehem in the beginning of barley harvest (Ruth 1:16,22). Beloved, let us love one another; for love is of God; and everyone that loveth is born of God, and knoweth God. He that loveth not, knoweth not God; for God is love (I John 4:7,8). By this shall all men know that ye are My disciples, if ye have love one to another (John 13:35). (Read I Cor. 13.)

PRAYER

Our Heavenly Father, grant us the gift of being a friend, than which there is nothing greater in the world. Let our love be Thy love shining through our imperfections, blessing and purifying us and all mankind. Amen.

THIRD DAY
THE FATHER WILL GIVE YOU IDEAS

First, if you wish to receive ideas, you must learn how to love the spirit behind the ideas. All great thinkers and great writers and great speakers loved ideas. Some, like Stevenson, carried notebooks in which they constantly jotted down the thoughts they especially liked as fast as they heard them. But all of them carried something more important than notebooks—they carried a love for the spirit behind the ideas.

Most of the great geniuses say that the Great Song has been already sung, and they merely tune in and let this Great Song sing through them. This was especially true of great poets—like Homer, Virgil, and Milton. But great scientists and inventors like Edison and George Carver have given voice to a very similar belief, when they asserted that their great discoveries flowed through them from the infinite forces in the universe.

But how does one "tune in" to this Great All Song? Homer and Virgil did it by "invoking the Muses." Socrates did it by consulting his "guardian angel" each morning before he started his day. Seneca always consulted his "genius."

We, today, take our inspiration from Jesus, who did not depend on "go-betweens" like "guardian angels" or "Muses," but who went straight to the Father in heaven whom He consulted in all things. Jesus knew that the spirit behind all ideas was the Great Idea-Bringer. When He left His disciples He told them that He would leave them the Spirit of Truth, Who would bring them into all truth.

Greater than Truth itself is this Power with which we can Conceive Truth, the Power with which we can Express Truth, the Power with which we can Create Truth. This is the Spirit of Truth which Jesus said He would leave with us, this is the Holy Ghost which He said would abide with us and dwell with us. If we love that Spirit of Truth it will unlock the gate of all wisdom and knowledge as fast as we need it. Love it and invoke it and watch the wonderful results. "Howbeit when He, the Spirit of Truth, is come, He will guide you into all truth: for He shall not speak of Himself; but whatsoever He shall hear, that shall He speak: and He will show you things to come." If you love the Spirit of Truth, you hold in your hands something more wonderful than the æolian harp of Jack of the Beanstalk, for you hold something by which you can draw ideas to you in the right way at the right time to make music for human souls.

Second, do you love the wholeness of the truth, or are you willing to accept only that part that fits in with your little particular theory? The scientific mind is the mind which throws over all theories and all hypotheses which do not square with the whole truth. The Wisdom of one age may be ignorance for the next. There was a day when the wise men believed the world was flat and stood still while the sun, moon, and stars revolved around it. There was a time, and that was only a short time ago, when doctors laughed at Pasteur when he said that invisible germs ten thousand times smaller than a flea could cause illness. Today there are some doctors (but mighty few really good ones) who laugh at the next great truth that is dawning upon mankind, that hate and fear and covetousness and greed and jealousy and envy—things that are ten million times smaller than a flea—are even more deadly than smallpox and diphtheria. Unless you are willing to accept the whole truth that the smaller and the more invisible a truth may be, the more powerful and germinating it can be, you cannot say that you are a true scientist, a true lover of truth.

What is true of the scientist is also true of the artist. He, too, must love the wholeness of truth. The true artist finds that anything that is seen in its completeness is always beautiful. Crack an English walnut so hard its "goodies" come forth in broken fragments and all beauty is destroyed. But tap it lightly and take the inside kernel out in all its completeness and the kernel is as beautiful as a butterfly wing. A cow, homely, awkward, clumsy, is a thing of beauty on canvas, but sliced up in beefsteaks, no art gallery would care for it. In the same way, if you could describe a personal experience in all its detail, no matter how trivial it might be, you might produce literature as perfect as the writings of Hawthorne or Dickens or Poe. If you can tell your whole experience of spiritual rebirth it may be as effective as changing souls as the testimony of Paul or Saint Francis or Brother Lawrence.

To be an artist, to be a scientist, to be a master of truth or a master expresser of that truth, train yourself to see each truth as a whole, to love all of it, and to express all of it when you speak or write or paint or dramatize it. He who loves all of truth will find all of truth coming to him.

Third, are you willing to pay the price?

Would you like to be a public speaker? Would you love to see yourself lecturing to great crowds of people? Would you love to have people applaud you and cheer you and lionize you? Would you love to receive the fame and glory and wealth that using such ideas will bring you? Or do you really and truly love great ideas for their own sake? Are you willing to work long and hard trying to build them up and arrange them in good sequence and in good climaxes?

If you are willing to pay the price for a thing, you have the right to pray for it, and only then. Henry Clay went out to the barn and gave addresses every day for two years to the cattle and pigs. He paid the price for his power as a speaker.

Would you love to be a famous pianist, but are not willing to pay the price for it in long hours and years over the piano? Paderewski said that if he did not practice six hours a day for one single day he knew the difference, if he missed two days his friends knew the difference, if he missed three days, his audience knew the difference.

Would you like to write novels like Dickens or plays like Shakespeare? Would you rather write than eat? Or is it merely the fame and glory and money you want?

In the same way, if you love ideas with all your heart and mind and soul—love them so much that you seek out libraries to read them, buy books that contain them, attend lectures where you can hear them, carry note-books to fill with them—if you love ideas like that, then you have a right to pray for them, and behold they will come to you, and nothing can stop them.

Fourth, are you willing to give these ideas away whenever or wherever they will be of value or will bring happiness to others? I had a friend who was a veritable store-house for humorous stories. No matter what was the place or the group, he always had a story that exactly fitted the occasion. And yet he did not hear any more stories than the rest of us. What was his secret? The first thing he did after he heard a funny story was to tell it to some one else, some one it would serve, delight, or amuse, or bring happiness to. When he came home in the evening he would entertain his family at dinner with the last story he heard during the day. The next day he would tell it to friends riding to the office in his street car.

Ministers are great collectors of ideas because every good idea they collect on week days they give to others on Sundays.

I made a great discovery years ago. I had been carefully husbanding a few ideas which I had carefully gathered for speeches. I dared not put them into books, because I was afraid I would not find any others so good to take their place for my lectures. But knowing that these ideas would bring happiness to others, I finally put them in books, and, to my surprise, immediately upon their publication a brand-new flood of ideas, far better than those I had given away, sprang full grown into my mind. This I find is always the case, in everything we do. Be generous, be prodigal in the giving, and great will be the receiving.

MEDITATION

Get wisdom, get understanding: forget it not; neither decline from the words of my mouth. Forsake her not, and she will preserve thee: love her and she shall keep thee. Wisdom is the principal thing; therefore get wisdom: and with all thy getting get understanding. Exalt her, and she will promote thee: she shall bring thee to honour, when thou dost embrace her. She shall give to thine head an ornament of grace: a crown of glory shall she deliver to thee (Prov. 4:5-9). If any of you lacketh wisdom, let him ask of God, that giveth to all liberally, and upbraideth not; and it shall be given him. But let him ask in faith, nothing wavering, for he that wavereth is like a wave of the sea driven with the wind and tossed.

For let not that man think that he shall receive anything of the Lord (James 1:5-7). (Read Job 28.)

Our Father, in whom are all the treasures of wisdom and knowledge hidden, unfold to us the right ideas at the right time, that we may become bearers of Thy light to bless and serve mankind. Amen.

FOURTH DAY

THE FATHER WILL GIVE YOU RICHES

If what you love loves you, then everyone who loves riches ought to become rich. But the trouble is that few people love riches in the right way.

First of all they should learn to love the inner spirit of wealth, the soul of riches.

The Soul of a thing is always a spiritual thing. Obtain that and you obtain all.

Once upon a time a farmer saw a great swarm of bees in a near-by woods. It occurred to him that it would be a nice thing to have bees on his farm so that he and his family could always have honey on their table. So he bought a hive and then went into the woods where he had seen the swarm, and caught a dozen or so bees and put them into the hive. The next day he caught a dozen more. At this rate he thought he would some day have enough bees to make all the honey he needed. But as fast as he caught them and turned them loose to gather honey for his hive, they went straight back—on a bee line— to the tree whence they came. In his perplexity he consulted a beekeeper. "What is the matter with these bees? Why don't they stay in my hive?"

"The only way to move a swarm of bees to your

place," said the beekeeper, "is to catch first of all the *soul* of the swarm. Once catch the soul and all the rest of the bees will come and abide with you. For where the soul is, there will the outer manifestation of the thing be also present."

"What is the soul of the swarm?" asked the farmer.

"The soul of the swarm is the queen. Catch her and all the rest of the bees, whose only object in life is to serve and give pleasure and profit to the soul of the swarm, will follow."

So we find the soul of a thing is the queen or the parent—usually the father-mother principle that holds all the rest of the thing together.

The parents of money are opulence and service. Service is the father of riches; opulence is the mother. When the soul and spirit of riches unite, riches come into manifestation. Money is here in this world for only two purposes—to flow in and to flow out in such a way as to create happiness for those who know how to use it; and the power that propels and initiates that circulation—both as a sending-forth power and as a drawing-in power—consists of *opulence* and *service*. Get these two spirits enthroned in your heart in happy marriage, and your riches will take care of themselves.

The reason why so few people in this world are rich is because so many people are either too selfish or too unselfish to draw money to them. This seems like a strange paradox, but it is very, very true. The unselfish people love service, the *spirit* of all true riches; but they do not love opulence, the *soul* of all true riches. Selfish persons love opulence, the mother principle behind all wealth; but they refuse to love service, the father principle behind all wealth. It is only when we take these two into our hearts and cherish them in equal measure—the soul and the spirit—the father and mother—that true wealth can come to us.

I know very well how completely you understand what I mean by service, and I know just as well how completely you misunderstand what I mean by opulence. Most of us think of service as something good and opulence as something bad. I understand that perfectly, because I, also, came from Puritan ancestry. There was a time when my forefathers thought that long, gloomy sermons were good, but stained-glass windows were bad. They thought that long, solemn prayers were good, but pipe organs and even singing of hymns were bad. And they thought that giving a hungry man a dish of soup was good, but that to give the same man, after his hunger was appeased, a book of beautiful poems was sentimental and foolish. I know people today who think a good dinner for a poor man is a great thing, but who think a beautiful painting for a yearning soul to gaze at is the height of impracticality.

I thought of using the word beauty in place of opulence, but beauty is not a strong enough word. God made a world with things to serve us, like potatoes and radishes and turnips. But He also gave us sunsets and rainbows and Grand Canyons and Niagara Falls. It takes my breath away when I start to enumerate the things that carry us so far beyond potatoes and radishes and turnips that the word beauty is not a great enough word for it. Such an infinite profusion of glory, such a wealth of color and grandeur, can only be adequately described by a word like opulence. Behold the glory of God's handiwork, the heavens, and how He has stretched them out before us.

If God made a world that goes beyond radishes and turnips, we should be willing to spend money for something besides radishes and turnips.

True, opulence in the hands of man has often been used for bad purposes—for mere selfish vainglory, for building cathedrals when people needed clothes, for buying pipe organs when children were starving. Service should always come first, but even on the authority of Jesus himself, opulence should not come far behind. Martha was giving service, while Mary, sitting on a comfortable stool at Jesus' feet, was reveling in the opulence of His presence. When service remonstrated with this spirit, Jesus Himself said, "Mary has chosen the better part." At another time another Mary broke precious ointment and poured it upon His feet, an act of opulence rather than of service, and when Judas rebuked her, saying the money spent on the ointment could better have been used for buying food for the poor, again Jesus said that opulence had done the better part. But in each of these cases there was the spirit of riches *in the heart* of the one expressing this opulence; it was *God's* beauty breaking through the actions of these women of earth.

Even though opulence has sometimes been used for bad and selfish purposes, is that any reason we should discard it and throw it aside? So, for that matter, has science been used for evil ends, so has philosophy, so has the church many, many times. Is that any reason we should brand science as an evil thing, or philosophy? Is that any reason we should leave the church and have nothing to do with it?

Even service has been many times misused because of our foolishness or short-sightedness. How many paupers have we made because we gave unwisely? How many grafters have we made by our prodigal spreading of largess? The entire organization of our Associated Charities with its "case system" and its scientific code of social science, sprang into being to correct the abuses that have grown out of our misuse of the great virtue of service. Opulence, if equally safeguarded, can be equally valuable for mankind. Opulence is not bad in itself. It merely has for most of us a bad connotation.

Let us see some of the things that are brought to us by opulence. It brings us beauty, harmony, ideality, loveliness, happiness, joy, breadth of view, wholeness, energy, efficiency, and love. What is wrong about having a beautiful home to match God's beautiful sunrise and sunset and mountains and lakes and streams? What largeness of soul creeps into children raised among beautiful scenes, large outlooks, lovely gardens, charming vistas? What is sinful about beautiful flowers in the front yard and beautiful books in the library? What is harmful in spending money for beautiful training in the arts so that the children can give beautiful expression to their souls in music, singing, dancing, so as to bring happiness to others? Opulence as a means of sending one's children to college, of taking them on a journey through Europe, and of giving them the graduate training they need to prepare them for the proper *service* that God intended them to bring to the world, is not an evil, but a good. All these things cost what most people call money. And what sin is there to love money and draw it to you for such beautiful twin purposes as service and opulence?

There is opulence in air-conditioning which makes the indoors partake of the health and wholesomeness of God's outdoors, but it is the opulence that builds peace and health and greater usefulness.

If you have two dollars more than is required for the actual needs of food, clothes, and shelter, spend one dollar for beauty, and give the other to the Associated Charities. The dollar you give for service helps some poor fellow who is out of a job; the other dollar you spend for opulence helps to keep another fellow from losing a job. They are the left and right hands of love. Bless both of them and hold these two hands upturned, consecrated, open, out to the Lord, and watch Him fill them with riches.

Second, do you love the whole of wealth?

Wealth consists of so many, many things that we fail to understand it if we limit it to dollars and cents. The man who recognizes wealth only in the form of money does not know it at all. Suppose you are going down the street, and just before you turn a corner you see the shadow of a woman on the walk and immediately fall in love with the shadow. You have never seen this woman, you never get an opportunity to see her, and yet you go through life saying that you are in love with her. Suppose that she has terrible features, that she is blind, or is deformed, or is deaf and dumb, or is insane, or is of a jealous, bitter, vindictive disposition, would you still love her? If you love wealth entirely in terms of dollars and cents you love only the shadow of wealth.

Wealth is more than dollars, it is more than houses and lands. It consists of the ideas within you, as yet unborn, which can be converted into many more dollars than you ever have earned before. It consists of an honest reputation which will enable you to borrow the money that will start your greatest business success. It consists of the happiness which you may obtain from simple things. What do you want money for, anyway? Is it not to buy happiness, buy ideas, buy culture, buy inspiration, beauty, freedom, wisdom, truth? And is it not possible for these things to come to you without the medium of any money whatever? Indeed, if one does not have the money for great opulence or great service, he must find his happiness and culture in simple things, for there is no worse way of breaking the moral law than in seeking a reputation for grandeur and generosity with borrowed money—with wealth that is not your own.

If you see wealth and love wealth in this larger aspect, you have a right to pray for it. But if your prayer for wealth is limited to praying for dollars and cents and stocks and bonds, then you have no more right to pray for wealth than the man has a right to propose marriage to the girl whose shadow alone he has seen.

Third, are you willing to pay the price for wealth?

If you love the inner spirit of wealth, and love the wholeness of it, it will come to you according to the measure of the price that you are willing to pay. The first price is the price of work, of industry, as is apparent to all. But the larger price is the willingness and capacity for taking this spirit of wealth—this wholeness of wealth, as I have been describing it to you—into your mind and heart and letting it fill you.

If you want immense wealth, millions of dollars of it, you will have to pay a large price. You may have to sacrifice your chosen life work in order to be transformed overnight into a philanthropist. Calls for help will start coming to you from all over the world—calls from which no man with a human heart and a sense of responsibility can bear to turn aside entirely. You will have to pay the price of meeting every week scores of people who will come into your life, not because they love you, but because they love your wealth and hope to receive some help from you. The moment a person becomes a rich man, cares like these multiply beyond belief. Are you willing to pay that price?

As one realizes that great wealth can be like a ball and chain bound around his ankles, he will be inclined to ask the Father to give him, not a million, but perhaps one hundred thousand instead, or, still better, a good job and a safe income, and let millionaires and others look after the philanthropic problems of the world. Do you want to spend the rest of your life in figuring out income taxes and clipping coupons, in looking after investments and reinvestments, in keeping track of the ups and downs of the investment market? Yes, are you willing to pay the price for great riches?

Fourth, are you willing to give money away?

I know scores of men who never became at ease financially until they started to tithe. The chief reason the Jews are the world's richest race is because of the centuries of tithing of their first fruits which disciplined their early history. The reason that the Mormon Church is the richest of all the world's churches today is because of the law of tithing which every Mormon faithfully observes. And I certainly know that the moment my wife and I determined to tithe of our at that time all too small professor's salary, we henceforth have never known the pinch of want.

When Mr. Baldwin, head of the Baldwin Locomotives, was going through his most perilous depressions and he had to borrow for his business, there was one item in his budget he never cut down, and that was his tithing. "This is my one safe investment," he told his associates when they begged him to cease giving away so much.

If you would rise above want, if you would increase your share of riches, you should resolve at once to build a definite plan of stewardship into your scheme of life, even before the money itself begins to come to you. "Dig your ditches."

MEDITATION

All Mine are Thine, and Thine are Mine (John 17:10). Give, and it shall be given unto you; good measure, pressed down, and shaken together, and running over, shall men give into your bosom. For with the same measure that ye mete withal it shall be measured to you again (Luke 6:38). My God shall supply all your need according to His riches in glory by Christ Jesus (Phil. 4:19). (Read Joel 2:21-27.)

PRAYER

Our Father, we thank Thee for the infinite abundance which Thou hast given to man. Help us to accept joyously that which Thou hast prepared for us with which to serve mankind and to glorify Thee. Amen.

FIFTH DAY
THE FATHER WILL GIVE YOU HEALTH

First. The first requirement for health is to love the spirit of health, which is wholeness. And behind wholeness is holiness. In other words, the way to have a healthy body is to love the body, but in a pure, holy, spiritual way.

I know a friend who always has good health, and who has great power in praying for the health of others. He has what I call a "matrix for health." He frankly loves the body. He thinks it is a beautiful thing. He sees it as the most wonderfully articulate thing that God has ever made. He loves to see people skate and dance and swim, and use their bodies rhythmically and joyously, for the glory of God and the happiness of man.

But he does not stop there. If he did he would be pure pagan. His healing power comes chiefly from the fact that he knows how to love the body in a spiritual way. He continually sees the bodies of himself and of his friends as expressions of the Spirit of God. To him our personal bodies are merely receiving sets for manifesting the messages of perfect love, truth, and joy of God through our channels of consciousness.

If one is sick he does not see a sick body, he sees merely a perfect receiving set catching a message from the great broadcasting station of God, and the moment the message is decoded and obeyed, instantly the sickness will vanish away. Is it not true that when you have answered the telephone call, the telephone bell ceases to ring? And is it not just as reasonable to believe that sickness itself is merely a vibration set up in the sensitive responses of our marvelously responsive body, which will cease as soon as we reverently put the receiver to our ear and promise to obey the command that is being sent?

I know, personally, that some of the most effective direct messages that God has ever sent me, He has sent in the form of temporary illnesses. One message was that I was to take more time to be still with Him. Another time He told me that I must throw out all of my worthless baggage of fears. When colds come to my friends I tell them that it is merely a private message from on High to cease being congested with the thought of self. Many of our ills might be traced to criticism or cynicism gone to seed—and so on and on. Indeed, I hardly know how I should get along in this world if it were not for the constant use of this marvelous receiving set for keeping me in continual touch with the steering hand of my Father in heaven. Since I have learned to look at it in this light I positively love my body.

Second, we must learn to love the whole of the human body.

The body is not only a receiving set for the catching of messages from the Broadcasting Station of God. It is the little microcosm of which the universe itself is the great macrocosm. In other words, the human body is the little outer expression in external, concrete, tangible form, of the inner, invisible, intangible qualities of God. Every organ of the body has a spiritual counterpart in the great soul of God. For example, the heart is but a spiritual manifestation of the Spirit of Love; the blood flowing through the veins and arteries is but the Spirit of Joy flowing through our channels of consciousness; our lungs represent the inbreathing and outbreathing of the Spirit of Life; the secretions of the liver represent the Spirit of Truth; and the action of the stomach symbolizes the receiving and the assimilating of the Spirit of Harmony and Power. Notice how quickly jealousy, anger and fear can poison and prejudice your viewpoint of Truth, and then notice how quickly they slow up and interfere with the actual digestive organs of your physical body as well.

When you begin to see the whole body, and love it, you will be amazed, not only to see how every organ, every nerve, every artery has an integral part in the health of your whole system, but how the body of your thoughts and emotions—your fear and faith, your jealousy and joy, your prejudice and pride, your laughter and love—

all manifest sooner or later in the health states of your body. To love all of your body means that you love all of the body of God—that is to say, all of His spiritual qualities. To do otherwise is to sin against the Holy Ghost.

To one who loves the body in this whole way, a wonderful healing secret becomes his. When he would help a weak heart he tells the patient to love more; to help a weak digestion he tells him to understand more; to help a weak circulatory system he tells him to express joy more.

Third, are you willing to pay the price for health?

Are you willing to make sacrifices for the health of your body? Do you refuse to poison your body with alcoholic drinks? Do you control your smoking within reasonable limits? Do you make yourself drunk on coffee and tea, or stuff your body with candy and sweetmeats at every opportunity?

Do you take calisthenics every morning? Do you take two miles on the hoof every day? Do you plan adequate rest periods, part of which time is communion with God? In short, do you love the body, the spirit of your body, your whole body to such an extent that you are willing to make sacrifices to keep it both whole and holy?

If you have paid the price in physical care you have paid only half. The greater half of sacrifice is the sacrifice of your wasteful emotions, such as fear, anger, and greed. If you are ever asked to pray for a person's health, you will learn, as I have learned, over and over again, the futility of your prayer unless the one for whom you pray cooperates in removing the life-destroying emotions that prevent the healing power of God from entering. If there are any hates or bitternesses, they must first be cast out before love can come in. If there are any fears, depressions, worries, glooms, they must first be removed before

joy can come in. Love and joy are the two greatest healing forces known to man; they so far surpass all other
medicines that science has produced, that there is no
comparison whatever. But you cannot buy these at the
corner drug store. They are the cheapest medicines in the
world, and yet to secure them one must pay the greatest
of all prices—the price of quiet meditation and prayer,
the price of wholesome loving and living—continued
faithfully for years and years.

Fourth, are you willing to give your health away?

It seems like a strange paradox to say that the way to
save your health is to spend it—to spend it as freely as
the need for it calls. While one should be willing to sacrifice his lower appetites and desires for the welfare of his
body, and to save and conserve his body by careful eat-
ing, exercise, and rest whenever possible, he need not
hesitate one instant in spending it freely and prodigally,
yes, even sacrifice it for any absolutely needful service for
others.

The moment another person is in danger, or is in serious need, one should cast aside all thought of self-preser-
vation, or self-protection and give himself without stint
and without limit. It is one of the greatest paradoxes in
the world that when the needs of others call upon one
the most, the health of the one who gives himself to their
needs, if done lovingly and joyously, is usually better
than ever. The explanation for this is that sickness of any
kind is merely congestion in some form—a stoppage
where there should be a melting and flowing. Unselfish
service is the most fluid thing we know; it is merely love
in action, it is love lifted to its most flowing and fluid
form. Add joy to this loving service and it becomes the
most healing, cleansing force in all the universe. Love is

the greatest thing in the world, and it forms the kernel and center of health. There can be no permanent health where love is not. But joy is the dynamic flowing power that carries this healing love to others. So the more one spends his body to help others, *lovingly* and *joyfully*, the healthier his own body actually becomes.

MEDITATION

I will restore health unto thee, and I will heal thee of thy wounds, saith the Lord (Jer. 30:17). Who healeth all thy diseases. Who satisfieth thy mouth with good things; so that thy youth is renewed like the eagle's (Ps. 103:3-5). (Read Mark 10:50-52.)

PRAYER

Our Father, give holiness to our Souls, wholeness and harmony to our thoughts and emotions, and health and healing to our bodies. Hold us close to Thee that we may become whole through and through, for we know that there is no health in us if we are separate from Thee. Amen.

SIXTH DAY

THE FATHER WILL GIVE YOU GUIDANCE

First, if you want God to guide your paths you must love the Spirit of Guidance. But what is the Spirit of Guidance? The Spirit of Guidance is Harmony. The only perfectly guided footstep is the footstep that is in harmonious relationship with all other footsteps. The only perfect plan for you is a plan that is in perfectly harmonious relationship with all other plans, and, above all, in perfect harmony with the great plan of God.

Hence, the first step in seeking guidance is to get perfectly still and calm within. As inner harmony begins to come to you, outer harmony will commence to manifest around you.

The best way to achieve that inner harmony is by looking at the perfect harmony of God in nature, in beautiful souls, and in His holy word. "Thou wilt keep him in perfect peace, whose mind is stayed on Thee, because he trusteth in Thee." "Acknowledge Him in all thy ways, and He shall direct thy paths." "Commit thy ways unto Him, trust also in Him, and He shall bring it to pass."

You can always tell when you are completely relaxed to God's guidance by the inner peace that comes to you. This inner peace will bring a joyous, creative urge that leads you into activity that unfolds your perfect plan; or it will bring a patience and stillness that will enable you to wait until others unfold the plan to you.

Second, you must love *all* of the plan that is yours, all of the guidance that comes to you. This plan may involve others, it may entail sacrifices, it may limit you as well as expand you. Can you love all of it and accept it in its entirety when it comes?

I have found that the part of the plan which people are most apt not to love, is not the inner hunch part, but the outer routine part. Never forget that guidance comes from without as well as from within. Sometimes it comes as a duty imposed upon us by our boss; an assignment by our teacher; a job by our dad. God has given us our parents, our teachers, our bosses—and a part of our guidance is not inspiration, but *obedience*. A man soon tires of riding a horse which will not obey his rein. How the Father must tire of guiding people who will not obey His commands. God's guidance will come less and less often to the one who refuses it when it does come. When one expects and prays for a big promotion God sometimes

sends a little promotion instead. He who is humble and
obedient enough to take the small promotion may be surprised to find later that this becomes a direct stepping-
stone to the higher promotion. It requires obedience and
humility, as well as inspiration and insight, to see and
follow all of God's guidance.

Third, are you willing to pay the price for guidance?.

What price must we pay for guidance? The price of
time spent in quietness and listening for the word or inspiration of God? That is one price, but that is a very,
very easy price—like sitting on a couch waiting for God
to do all of the work. We also have some work to do.
While we are waiting for God to do His share, we must
get busy and do our share. But what do we mean by
God's share and our share?

God's share is to put the future into order for us, and
present it to us in perfect pattern. Our share is to put the
past into order and accept with radiant acquiescence (or
at the very least with patient resignation) all of the seeming disappointments and failures of the past. When you
comb your hair you do not look at the hair on your head
and comb it; you comb the hair in the mirror. By some
strange miracle, easy to accept because of long custom,
you find that the hair on your head becomes combed by
that process. In the same way sit down and put your past
in order, and you will be amazed how God instanta-
neously commences to put the future in order.

But how can one put one's past in order? How does
this process of putting one's plans in order have any
similarity with combing one's hair in the mirror?

They are almost identical. You know that there is no
time in heaven, there is nothing but eternity. There is no
past there, and no future—only the eternal Now. And

this eternity is never broken into fragments like minutes and seconds and hours, but exists eternally as an infinite whole. There is no past apart from the future, and no future apart from the past. Neither are there any fragments of events existing in heaven; every event is a part of the Whole Event, of which all little actions are a part. Therefore, if we should like to assist God to put the future (which we have not seen) into a perfect pattern, it behooves us to sit down before the past (which we have seen) and do our share in putting it into as perfect a pattern of harmony as we know how.

That means that we must erase from our hearts all self-pity for the bumps we have received. We must see in our disappointments God's appointments. It means that we must forgive and forget the wrongs that have been done to us by others, seeing in every kick we receive a boost upwards to something better. It means that we must correct those mistakes of our own making, if there still remains time in which to correct them. It means that we must make restitution, wherever it is humanly possible, for our misdeeds; and where we cannot make restitution to one we may have hurt, we must make it in the form of some good deed done for some other whom some one else has hurt. Finally, we must thank God for the past as it is, giving the gratitude that has long been overdue, to the One to whom gratitude belongs.

Fourth, you must give guidance away.

The way to give guidance away is to sit down with your neighbor when he comes to you asking guidance, and help him plan his future and prayerfully pass these ideas of guidance on to him. The way to give guidance away is to share your quiet time with others when you think it would help them, and spend as much time in praying that God helps them as you spend asking Him to help you. It is remarkable how much clearer one's own path becomes after spending an hour unselfishly and lovingly in trying to help another find *his* path.

But the biggest way of giving guidance away is to be perfectly willing to relinquish your divine plan, or at least your own conception of your divine plan, if at any time it seems that God so wills it. For if it *is* God's plan for you, nothing can take it permanently away, and if it is a mistaken conception of what your plan should be, the quicker you let go of it the better. By this act of relinquishment you are giving God all of the power, the complete control of your life, so that nothing will hinder His bringing your plan into complete fulfillment.

And as you relinquish it, peace comes to you. Peace is the proof that your prayer is answered. "Our cargoes always come to us over calm seas." God's perfect plan never fails to manifest itself to the man who carries a peaceful soul.

MEDITATION

In all thy ways acknowledge Him, and He shall direct thy paths (Prov. 3:6). (Read Ps. 5.)

PRAYER

Our Heavenly Father, guide our ways and lead us gently in the path that is to be ours. Lighten our path and direct our steps. Hold us in Thy divine plan. Amen.

SEVENTH DAY

THE FATHER WILL GIVE YOU WORLD PEACE

First, to attain world peace we must love and work to attain in our own souls the *inner spirit* of peace. Before we can attain harmony of nations we must attain harmony of individuals. That harmony must begin in each individual soul. If we love that inner peace of mind in our own and in other souls, then we have a right to pray for peace, and only then. When Jesus said, "Blessed are the peacemakers, for they shall be called the children of God," He was referring to those who create peace in individual souls just as much as to those who bring peace to nations.

Even though nations should agree on a scrapping of all navies and armaments, and putting a complete end to the disease called war, unless this inner peace is attained, the disease will break forth in other and equally disastrous forms—in drunkenness, immorality, or the seven plagues of Egypt.

Yes, changing individual lives must precede, be one step ahead, of every effort to change nations, if we would have that change permanent.

Second, in visioning world peace we must take into consideration all that is involved in economic, educational, and religious cooperation. Above all, we must see the necessity of curbing national greed, even to the extent, if necessary, of abolishing the entire profit system through the duration of the war, not only in regard to munitions, but also in regard to the production and handling of steel, cotton, oil, coal, and other requisites of war. Indeed, the achieving of world peace may require a great International Social Planning Agency, with its center in Switzerland or at The Hague. Are we able to take in the significance of world peace in its entirety? But this leads us to the next and most difficult question to answer.

Third, are we willing to pay the price? Are the "have got" nations willing to share colonies, and free access to raw materials, with the "have not" nations? Are the white nations willing to give parity and freedom to the dark nations? Will the strong nations agree to stop exploitation of the weaker nations?

Will America be willing to sit in a World Court, in a League of Nations, and participate in an international "policing" system, to enforce order and law in a United States of the World? If the nations of the world undertake a whole and complete program in a real and sincere approach toward world peace, will we be willing to pay the price of pooling our resources and power to bring it to pass? Will we as individuals, by keeping daily prayer periods, be willing to do our best toward paying the price of inner discipline to achieve peace in our own souls, and help achieve in other souls a peace that will lead to a true spiritual awakening and rebirth in our nation, that will insure and guarantee permanence to the outer peace? If religious folk will be willing to pay that price, then we have the right to pray for world peace.

Fourth, are we willing to give the peace away? Are we willing to put our major emphasis upon preaching the inner changing of individual souls? Are we willing to put, even before peace, the changing of materialistic greed to a social conscience, national pride to national justice, and racial inferiority to racial cooperation? If we are willing that peace shall wait upon such changes, if God so wills, then we have the right to pray for peace. Then world peace is nearer at hand than we imagine.

MEDITATION

But in the last days it shall come to pass, that the mountain of the house of the Lord shall be established in the top of the mountains, and it shall be exalted above

the hills; and people shall flow unto it. And many nations shall come, and say, Come, and let us go up to the
mountain of the Lord, and to the house of the God of Ja-
cob; and He will teach us of His ways, and we will walk
in His paths: for the law shall go forth of Zion, and the
word of the Lord from Jerusalem. And He shall judge
among many people, and rebuke strong nations afar off;
and they shall beat their swords into plowshares, and
their spears into pruninghooks: nation shall not lift up a
sword against nation, neither shall they learn war any
more. But they shall sit every man under his vine and under his fig tree; and none shall make them afraid: for the
mouth of the Lord of hosts hath spoken it (Micah 4:1-4).
(Read Gen. 32,33.)

PRAYER

*Our heavenly Father, awaken in the souls of men the spirit
of love that was in Christ Jesus. Bring justice into the courts
of nations. May the spirit of cooperation take the place of
competition and greed. Raise up men in industry and gov-
ernment who are so filled with the spirit of the Christ that
the Prince of Peace may work through them to bring peace on
earth, good will to men. Amen.*

INTERLUDE

After this week of praying on the mountain top, one
can apply this "love way" of prayer to any problem, either individual or national. After praying for world
peace, one might just as easily turn his prayers to the li-
quor problem, capital and labor, inter-racial relations, the
Church, foreign missions, national prosperity, govern-
mental efficiency and integrity.

At this point, however, I must warn you that this book

is not a book of methods. The reader may be tempted to read it through hastily for the *ideas* that it contains. He may try to apply these as *rules*, without stopping to go through the process of silence and meditation which the daily studies are meant to encourage. This book only serves its purpose as it provides channels for opening up a new spiritual relationship for the reader—a quickened insight, a purified devotion and an inner contact with God, not heretofore attained.

Out of periods of meditation and of prayer, faithfully observed over a period of months, there will come certain uprushes or inrushes of intuition, unexpected and unexplainable solutions to old problems, new creative attitudes toward persons and events, which will make life a richer, happier, and more heavenly experience.

After one has finished reading this book he will know what the author has written there. But if he is patient enough to spend another month upon it, he may discover what he himself has written, unconsciously, between the lines and along the margins. If he reads it a third time, he may find what God has written into it—through the unseen orchestration of author and reader.

V

Parables That Come to Pass

 From the moment that the first chapter of *The Soul's Sincere Desire* appeared in the form of an article in the *Atlantic Monthly* in August, 1924, until now I have been continually asked for examples of answered prayer as drawn from my own life and experience. One day I started to make an extended reply to this request in the way of a long list of concrete examples, but I had not gone far before I realized that I was giving only one portion, and that the smallest and least important portion, of the "miracle," the outside portion, the portion in which I was the least interested in having my readers get. It was like giving to men who had come seeking seed corn the mere outer shells or husks. All those who have read my little book, *The Soul's Sincere Desire*, will know that to me a miracle of any kind is merely the external manifestation of something very precious that has transpired within the most sacred chambers of the inner soul. The greatest difficulty which I have had to face when sharing my experience with others is in making the rank and file accept this viewpoint and make it central in their lives.

From time immemorial, the moment the inner spirit clothes itself in tangible, objectified, externalized form, that moment the vast majority cease to look at the true reality—the inner essence—which is the real *cause* of all, and turn their attention to the external appearance, which is merely the *effect*. It is easy to forget that the life is more than the food and the body than the raiment. The true glory and majesty and magnificence attend, not the loaves and fishes, but the *compassion* with which the Christ looks upon the multitude. And yet how rarely does one hear the word *compassion* discussed when a group of good people get together to discuss the miracle of the feeding of the five thousand! How often the attention is centered entirely upon the word *multiplication*! Yet put these words side by side and how thin and tawdry the latter word sounds before the first—how mechanical, cold, and trivial! The world could very easily have lived a thousand years without knowing the word multiplication, but it could not live one day if compassion were taken out of it. *The real miracle, the greatest miracle, in this world is that a man can love another.* Indeed, is not the word *multiplication*, as applied to the biological unfoldment of our human race, dependent upon the word *love*? And turning from the biological to the artistic, educational and religious developments of our race—how increasingly great the word *love* looms in our lives! Yes, the life is more than the food, and the body than the raiment.

How much effort Jesus expended in cautioning His disciples to beware of the leaven of the Pharisees, who were always looking for an outward sign! Ye can read the signs of the times, but ye cannot read the greatest sign of all—the sign of love written large in the human heart.

And when the disciples came back enthusiastic after their first missionary tour, and all began to talk at once, so eager were they to tell of the wonderful, external, concrete results of their prayers for the sick and the sinning, He quickly rebuked them, saying, "Notwithstanding, in this rejoice not, that the spirits are subject unto you; but rather rejoice because your names are written in heaven." Rejoice not that you have effected union with the things that perish; rejoice, rather, that you have established union with love that is eternal. The wonderful thing that has happened to you is not that you are able to bring to pass miracles in the external world, miracles that you can apprehend and prove to yourself with your five senses; the wonderful thing that has happened to you is that you have at last found that your God is a God of Love and Compassion, whom you may passionately love with all your strength and with all your soul and with all your heart and with all your mind.

External results from prayer have a value only as figures in a bankbook have a value in informing the world that you have gold deposited in the bank. If you did not have the gold in the bank, the figures would mean nothing. And if you have the gold but can not recall the figures, the gold will still be there. If the miracle did not happen, God would still be in His heaven. Bankbooks and miracles are not the only way to prove that there is gold on earth and a God in heaven. They just happen to be convenient, and for most people exceedingly popular ways of conveying this information. Even Jesus recognized their practical importance when He said, "By their fruits ye shall know them."

However, Jesus Himself was very reticent about spreading abroad the reports of the external results of His inner prayer life. How often we read after something especially striking had happened, "He cautioned them that they should tell no man!" His reason for this, it seems to me, was His deep inner intuition that all people are not at the same time at the same level of spiritual unfoldment. The kind of treatment necessary for the growing grain is not, for instance, what is needed for the ripened corn.

The food for the grown-up may be too strong for the little child. Most of the people about Him were in the childhood of spiritual evolution, not ready yet to see through the outer husk to the inner spirit. Therefore He must dole out very carefully the outer miracles or clothe them in forms that would be more easily assimilative to their souls.

The form He used most frequently to convey spiritual truths to the unripened mind was the parable. By this method He could keep the inner experience concealed from those whose hearts were hardened and unprepared like untilled soil is hardened and unprepared for the planting. Yet at the same time the parable shell was adapted for holding all the essence of the truth hermetically sealed, so to speak, and as safely preserved as a grain of corn preserves within itself the germ of new life, ready for instant immolation and growth the moment the soil opens to receive it.

When requests come to me to tell some of the miracles of answered prayer that have fallen within my own experience, I naturally turn to this vehicle which was so frequently used, and so blessed in its use, by Jesus the Christ. The twelve "parable miracles" that follow may be read by those who so desire as so many pretty little fairy stories to gladden the heart and brighten an idle hour. To others they may be accepted for just what they are—true accounts of actual happenings, in which the events have been minimized and understated rather than overstated. But for all who read them they are intended as seeds to be planted as rapidly as the soil is made ready to receive them. It is trusted that from this simple planting may come forth a harvest of grain either now or in the days to come—grain that may furnish food for the very bread of life, bread that may be assimilated unto oneself and become bone of one's bone and flesh of one's flesh—bringing additional strength to some who may need it, some who may be facing long days and nights of weary travel along life's hard pathway.[1]

1

THE PARABLE OF THE STARS IN THEIR COURSES

One evening there were gathered together some men, all of whom were interested in the virtue of prayer, and one of them told to the others this incident:

"I had been standing on a street corner, waiting for a bus, when it occurred to me that when one has nothing else to do, power, instead of being dissipated by impatient longing, might be stored up by turning the thoughts to God and realizing the Kingdom in all the changing aspect of things.

"So, standing there, I looked about me, ready to see in the varied pictures passing before me the perfect harmony of God's perfect unfolding plan.

"I saw then two middle-aged women on the other side of the street, coming from opposite directions and destined to pass each other right opposite me. 'As truly as God governs the stars in their courses,' I thought to myself, 'just as surely will He keep these women in their courses so they will meet and pass without collision and without accident.' I watched them pass each other and I let my thoughts pass on with them as they disappeared into the 'infinite space,' realizing that each was going on a necessary errand, perhaps for her loved ones, and that

---

[1]The parables that follow may be used for daily meditations if the reader so desires.

each errand would be fulfilled with perfect joy and harmony, without accident of any kind.

"But as I turned my eyes in another direction I beheld a different sight. A little girl in the yard was saying sharp and angry things to a little boy on the sidewalk and he was retaliating with still more angry vigor. 'How does this harmonize,' I asked myself, 'with the harmony with which stars are governed in their courses without collision or discord of any kind?' Then I realized suddenly that such discord did not belong in the picture at all, either in infinite spaces or in our smaller spaces. I found myself watching them with surprise, astonishment, and unbelief, placing them in my thoughts with the stars in a benign pattern of infinite order. As I was thinking this, the boy turned on his heel and slowly crossed the street, and as he did so a look of the tenderest remorse that I have ever witnessed on a child's face came over it. I looked back to the little girl, and on her face almost the same transformation occurred. She started to reach out her hand as though to call him back, but let it fall reluctantly to her side, and, with eyes on the verge of tears, turned back to her play. The little boy had now reached the opposite side of the street and he too had turned and was looking back at the girl, whose attention now was on her play. He stood there with those deep, sad eyes for several minutes as though hesitating whether to cross over and make amends for what he had done or said. But I, who had seen it all, knew that he had already been forgiven. He turned then and passed on.

" 'It is well,' I thought. 'They are in God's hands. They will meet again at school or in play and the deep lesson of cooperation and comradeship and self-control will bear fruit, perhaps a hundredfold, giving them lasting protection against such clashes for the rest of their lives.'

"For myself, I had learned as great a lesson as they. For I knew now that to vision infinite order is to create finite order, for we are patterned after the stars, and woven in the warp and the woof of their being and take our order from them, wearing here below miniature designs of a great pattern so that the smallest atom is a little sun, partaking of the virtue of its parenthood. As the atom builds itself upon the infinite wisdom of the planetary system, so would we use the law to create for ourselves a finite order which in the scope of its perfect action would be infinite.

"My bus came, but the time had passed as quickly as though I had been standing on the threshold of the Kingdom of Heaven."

2
THE PARABLE OF THE POSITIVE AND NEGATIVE RAY

That same evening another spoke to the same men and related this experience:

"A friend of mine had for sale two little cottages. She had need to dispose of these cottages, for her happiness lay elsewhere, so she had proceeded in the usual way and had put the matter into the hands of real-estate agents. A buyer was found, but in the end he would not pay the one thousand dollars down which was required by my friend.

" 'How do you know,' I said to her when she expressed her disappointment to me—'how do you know that this prospect would be happy in buying your property?' For I thought that for the property there must naturally be buyers. So I spoke further to her.

" 'The physicists maintain that there is no negative-poled atom in the universe but has its corresponding positive ray somewhere in infinite space, even if it be a million miles away, and that nothing in heaven or in earth can prevent their ultimately finding each other out. Is it not reasonable to believe that there is a similar law prevailing in the relations of man to man, and that when one has a beautiful thing to dispose of, another, somewhere, even though he be thousands of miles away, can be made happy by that very thing; and that, if we but trust all to God, we might find that nothing on land or sea could prevent the supply and the need from finding each other?'

"She was much struck by my talk and let the matter drift for a few days while she thought what was best to be done.

"It was only a few days later that a friend of mine who lived some two thousand miles away came to my door. He was enthusiastic about the little city and exclaimed almost immediately, 'If I could secure a position on the city newspaper, I should like nothing better than to buy a few little cottages to rent and settle down here for life.'

"A week later he told me that he had been successful in getting the position on the paper and asked me to help him find a couple of cottages which might be for sale.

"When I showed him the cottages of my friend he was delighted with them. When I told him the price he protested that it was too small. When I asked him what he could pay down he replied without hesitation, 'One thousand dollars.'

"I brought the prospective buyer and seller together and as I sat in the room I was witness to one of the most extraordinary business conversations that was ever held.

They argued, the buyer wanting to pay more, the seller to take less! At last a settlement was reached. They both took up their lives each benefited by the mutual transaction. I felt somehow as if in the exchange even of that piece of what is commonly called 'real estate' there had been an exchange of some subtle and penetrating law of need and fulfillment, through which their lives became more blessed."

3

THE PARABLE OF THE LIGHT THAT SHONE IN THE DARKNESS

One day a man received a letter. And this is what the letter said:

"Because something you said helped me to see the light and because it brought me great comfort when trouble was thick upon me, I am coming to you again for help. This time my little daughter, my only child, is attacked by illness which the doctors say cannot be stopped, but will prove fatal. In my anxiety and despair, I am turning to you for help. I trust all to your prayer."

For a little while this letter troubled the man. Here was one leaning upon him for something he knew he could not give. Nevertheless, knowing that the need was great, he sat down and wrote the man as follows:

"Step off the top of a ten-story building and give yourself without question to the air, knowing that the parachute will open and save you. As the air is all about you and is sufficient to support the parachute, so God's love is all about you and is sufficient to support my prayer. I shall pray for you. Love will be in my prayer. Step into the atmosphere of divine love and give yourself unresistingly to its power."

As he wrote, and even as the carrier went off with the

letter, the man ceased to think of the stranger who had written him, but thought rather of the infinite trust which could fill a man's soul, who would have written him for help as this one had done; and as he thought, it seemed to him that the one who had written him faded out of sight and where he had stood before, nothing but light remained, the clear, bright light of trust, and then he knew that trust was one of the greatest things in the universe. For trust is something which no manner of evil can hurt, for it is just like the air: when the sword cleaves it, it gathers together again; when one would destroy it, he finds it cannot be touched. Trust cannot be exhausted, for the more it is used, the stronger it grows; and the more it is reviled the more impervious and indestructible it becomes. No impurities or weaknesses can find a lodgment in trust any more than darkness can find a foothold in light. When light enters a room, darkness runs out of the door. When trust fills a man, evils flee from his being— yes, out through his very pores. Trust is impenetrable by anything which is unlike itself, just as light is impenetrable by darkness. It is impervious to all thrusts of those who would destroy it, and yet it enslaves and binds and limits no man who surrenders himself captive unto it.

Thus the petitioning friend faded out of the man's vision and in his place he saw only trust. Where he stood all shadows of darkness had vanished and there stood only light. And thus having written and thus having sat and thought awhile the man was interrupted by pressing demands and went off and forgot the matter entirely. A few days later a letter came from the one who had been in trouble, saying that his daughter had miraculously become that very hour both sound and well, that other beautiful blessings had come into his home, that his business had commenced to prosper, and that his God had commenced to do his thinking for him.

Then it was that a great wonder came to the man, for experiences like this were at the time new to him. Is escape from the evils that beset us as simple as that? he asked. Can a man be made whole by his faith alone? Can all darkness vanish from a room by the simple act of turning on the light?

4

THE PARABLE OF DANIEL IN THE LION'S DEN WITH HIS HANDS TIED, THE DOORS LOCKED, AND THE WILD BEASTS UPON HIM

A man who was in great trouble said to his wise friend, "I do not know which way to turn. I am without hope. Every misfortune has come upon me."

And his friend said to him, "You are Daniel in the lion's den, with your hands tied, and the ravening beasts about you. But take courage, for it is in such moments that God is most imminent, His power most marvelous and the answer to prayer most certain. For so long as there remains one door which our human eyes can light upon as a means of escape, then we, in our ignorance, act in our own willfulness rather than through God's will. You who are in despair abandon yourself to God, you cease to speak for yourself in arrogant manner, but become as a child and give yourself over as a child to the Divine Father. Thus your hopelessness gives you liberty. So it is with a child who falls from the highest place and breaks no bones while a man falling from the same height is crushed and mutilated. With the one it gives itself to the air, knowing no fear, and is unhurt and well, while the other, being conscious of himself rather than of

God, thinks, as he is falling, 'I will cleverly save myself,' and thus he is dashed to pieces below.

"You are wounded only in so far as you resist. For nothing exists in the universe to harm you save as you oppose yourself to it, making it alien to you; on the other hand, the wildest beast is but a sheep of your Father's. Put your trust in that Shepherd and you and the beast that threatens you will dwell together in His bosom."

And he ended, saying, "Go now and you will be taken care of; we do not know when or how it will come, but it will come."

And the man went and the next day came again, but this time with a face radiant, and cried out joyfully to the wise man that, as if by miracle, the tangled skein of his troubles had overnight been unraveled and put again in perfect order and that he had indeed been saved as Daniel from the wild beasts that had beset him.

5

THE PARABLE OF THE MAN WHO FOUND THE ELIXIR OF YOUTH

A man came to another and said, "I am growing old. My limbs are not so supple as they used to be. My mind is becoming stiff and ideas no longer come easily to me as they used to. I dread old age. Why cannot we stay forever young?"

"We can," said the other.

"Tell me how," exclaimed the first one, "for if you have an elixir of eternal youth I would share it with you."

"When you were young did you ever admire a teacher?"

"I did," replied the other.

"Did you ever admire a teacher so much that you tried

to walk like he did, talk like he did, form your opinions like he did?"

"Yes, many teachers I admired like that."

"And after you walked, talked, and thought like him for many days, did you grow more like him or less like him?"

"More like him."

"And were all your teachers older than yourself."

"Yes, all."

"So in becoming like the older people you admired and took for your models, you grew like those you admired. In the past you admired age and took it for your guide. Now go and change your teachers awhile."

"What do you mean?"

"Go and take a little child for a teacher, learn of him. Turn and become like a little child. Look out upon life as though you had never seen it before. Let every sunset be the first sunset you ever saw, and every sunrise be for you the beginning of a new day of marvels and miracles. Look out upon life with eyes of wonder. Don't use over and over again old, worn-out opinions that thousands have used and discarded before you. Form a new spontaneous conception for every joy that comes to you. Don't define and catalogue each experience—live and enjoy every experience."

And the man went on his way, and he took children for his playmates, and his joints grew more supple and his mind more pliant and keen; but the greatest good fortune of all that came to him was the discovery that he could now see the little child in every man he met; in the most confirmed sinner he could see the innocent soul; through the deepest blackness he could catch the glimmer of Light. Thenceforth he knew that never in this world nor in the world to come would he ever know what old age was. For he had found the spring of eternal youth and he would never again let it get away from him.

6

THE PARABLE OF THE THREE MEN
WHO LOST WHAT THEY WANTED

There came three men to the home of an old man, and they said, "We are all very unhappy because we lost what we wanted." One of them was especially bitter as he spoke.

"I am through with prayer," he said. "I prayed hard for a victory, and instead of coming to me it went to my bitterest enemy."

The old man replied, "Was it a victory you needed?"

And the bitter friend said, "Oh, I didn't *need* it, but I *wanted* it."

The other asked, "Did you want the victory perhaps that you might give to those you love?"

But the man answered: "No, I didn't want it for that. I wanted it so that I should take it from my rival. I prayed for that and my rival won it. I am through with prayer."

The older one said, "But I always thought, myself, that prayer was asking for a gift in love. I should think that hate and rivalry would blight the prayer as the cold does flowers, that it would kill the precious gift of the spirit as Herod killed the infants in order that he might slaughter the one with the divine spirit."

But the man was a closed door and a barrier to these words and only answered, more bitterly: "I am through with prayer. After this when I want a thing I'll go out and get it."

And then, because his business was pressing and his

mind was filled with many things to be done, he said farewell to his friends and hurried on his way.

And the gentle one knew that the other was closing the door against all that might help him and that henceforth he would have to fight, alone, the bare and brutal physical world without the ointment of the divine upon him, for he knew that now he was a wall and not a channel for a message to pass through him. So he turned to the two, leaving the other in the hands of the Divine Father, who touches the blind as well as those who see; and the man was at peace, for he knew that in the mysterious ways of divinity that which is a wall will become a door, that which is closed will open, and the barrier will become a channel.

Then one of the two men who had remained said: "Tell me further of this. I too prayed for a victory which was denied, but I prayed not for myself alone, but for one I love. Tell me why my prayer was not answered."

"I have yet to find when a prayer is asked in love," replied the other, "that a door ever closes, but there is a sign upon it, if one can but see it, pointing to a better door further on ahead. I never yet found a road obstructed where there was not another and a better road if we turn to the right. When the door to the Senatorship was shut for Abraham Lincoln, was it not merely a sign that the door of the Presidency was ahead?"

"But," asked the man, "how can one be sure he can *see* that other door?"

"I shall explain that to you by a parable," replied the other.

"Upon the day when she was seven, a little girl was given a party to which were invited twelve of her friends.

As they all sat around the table before the dainty refreshments and the cake with seven candles, the little girl's father, thinking to surprise her, brought in a plate of gingerbread. But the little girl soon saw that there were only twelve pieces of gingerbread, and she set to wondering avariciously how these would go around to thirteen people, and it occurred to her that as she was the hostess her father would probably pass her by, and being a selfish little girl she became full of stinging jealousy and she even thought dark thoughts about her father for providing only twelve pieces of gingerbread instead of thirteen. She became so jealous and angry that she soon began to cry.

"She had forgotten that her father knew very well that she did not care at all for gingerbread. Her thoughts were so taken up with the slight she had received from one to whom she looked always for what she wanted, that she did not see her father come in with a heaping plate of angel-food cake. Her father, always thinking of her, knew that instead of gingerbread his little girl dearly loved angel-food cake. But the foolish child was so blinded by tears over her imagined wrong that she had no eyes for her real good, so that after a while the other children, thinking that she did not care even for cake, divided her piece up among themselves and ate all to the last crumb."

And he who asked rose to his feet.

"I understand," he said, and went on his way.

Then the only one who remained turned to the old man and said, "It is easy for one to see this with one's mind, but it is hard to see it with one's heart. Can you help my heart to see?"

"If I could only make your heart see," replied the old

man, "then when your prayer is not answered in exactly
the way you want to have it answered, you would actually *rejoice* that you had been denied."

The young man, being incredulous, asked him how it
was possible to rejoice when he had been denied, and the
old man instructed him further:

"When I pray, there are limits to what is possible to my
eyes. When my small prayer is not answered in the way I
would expect it, I know that the answer will be without
limit, boundless, beyond my asking, coming only from
the power whose beneficence is beyond imagining."

And the young man said, "But there are certain things
one wants. And one wants them one's own way."

And the old man with patience spoke further: "I am
old and my physical eyes see but a little way. You are
young and you see great distances in the world. But because I am old, with the dimming of my outward sight
has come the brightening of my inward vision. And I see
that prayer cannot be answered except as you give yourself to its will and abide in joy by its fulfillment. Prayer is
the gift of divine love, it is the sacrament between God
and man. You do not take ruthlessly of your human love,
but you give to it abundantly and abandon yourself to its
will; then can you neither take nor command divine love,
but must abide in its will and give yourself wholly to its
beneficent power.

"So sure has become my faith in this love of God that I
abide in it without question. When my human prayer is
not answered in the way I would expect to have had it, I
am exalted, for I know I have submitted to a will greater
than my own and capable of infinitely more goodness.

"When a man is in love he does not then exist alone.
How much more is it true that if a man dwells in divine

love he cannot exist alone, but is dependent and interdependent upon that love. I live upon it as I live upon air; with as much faith, for I know it will keep me with life even after the air of our earth has become nothing. I ask of it and I know that I ask not of my enemy who is separate from me, but that I ask of my Father.

"I have faith in His wisdom. It may appear to my eyes hard, but I know how little vision the eyes have. For He said unto us, Rejoice, little children, that you have a heavenly Father who, when you ask for a stone will give you bread, and when you ask for a scorpion will give you meat."

And the young man said, "Thank you for speaking to my heart. Now I too understand." And he rose and went on his way.

7

THE PARABLE OF THE FOUNTAIN THAT WAS ETERNAL

There was once a teacher of young people. He spent his days telling them of the craft of writing, but it seemed to him that he failed. He did not know the reason for his failure. But it seemed to him that he had before him great treasures and that, through blindness or ignorance, he could not touch them deeply enough, that he could not find in them the living fountains of creation.

After they had all gone away he would sit alone, wondering how he could mine deep enough to strike living waters in them. He remembered the earth, so heavy, upon which they all walked. He remembered how they knew, and their very lives depended upon the knowledge, that far below the thick crust of soil was flowing, secret and powerful, the living waters of the earth. And while he was thinking there came to him visions of his boyhood. It happened that where he lived there were two ways of gaining access to these vital waters—one was by a pump, which had to be primed and gave forth water only after great exertion; the other was by an artesian spring which never needed priming, but gave its water freely from the depths of the earth.

And it seemed to him as he meditated that he had been priming pumps and that that was the reason for his failure. At the same time he knew that, as in the earth, so in his pupils there must be deep founts of living waters of creation, which if only discovered would yield up vast riches. He took new heart and determined to find, if he could, the access to these waters.

He no longer went to the shallow surface water which needed priming, for he was in search of artesian wells. He hunted long, and he wrote down his observations on the way, so that others might follow him and found their works, like the cities of old, by the deepest wells. He put these things into books, and other teachers, who, alone and weary, had searched also, read them and went, too, in search of deep wells.

His students became creators of living works. The wells, when found, became no longer wells, but actual fountains, and an eternal flow of living water sprang up around him.

8
THE PARABLE OF THE MAN WHO GAVE AWAY
THE ONE HE LOVED

A young man came to a friend he could trust and said to him, "The girl I love has asked to be set free. What shall I do?"

"Let her be free," replied the other, quietly.

"But I love her so," cried the other. "How can I bear to give her up?"

"How much do you love her?"

"More than any woman has ever been loved by any man in all the world."

"Even then you do not love her enough," replied the other, "otherwise you could give her up when she asks it. What you call love is mere attachment. When a mother loves her son so much that she cannot bear to have him far enough out of her sight for him to go away to college, or go away to the Senate, or go away to find his great life plan, then she does not love him enough. When a wife cannot let her husband take a journey that will bring to him his great opportunity, it is not her love that holds him, but her attachment. Let your love be colossal enough to give your loved one away to her great destiny, her great life plan. Give her to anything which will make her happier than you can make her—if there is anything in the world that can do it. Can you love her enough—in your heart of hearts—to do that?"

And the young man bowed his head, and his lips moved as though in prayer. Then he said, while his eyes gleamed with a new sad brightness:

"I *can*."

Months rolled by, and again the young man came to his friend, and this time his face was shining, and his eyes had a new and deeper radiance in them than his friend had ever seen before.

"Share my happiness, dear friend, for I am in heaven," he said. "I gave my beloved away. I gave her to destiny, I set her eternally free. She went her way and entered into her freedom. A few days later she came back to me, and this is what she said:

" 'All my life I have been seeking for such a love as you have just been giving to me, and I knew it not—a love that is great enough to forget itself in seeing its loved one completely happy. That kind of love is the kind I thought only the angels could give. I did not know there was such love anywhere outside of heaven. Had I known it I should have sought it long ago. Now that I know it exists I cannot cease till I find it and make it my own. So take me, keep me forever.' "

And he went his way, and as his friend watched him go he thought in his heart, "There goes the love that holds the planets in their places."

9

THE PARABLE OF THE WELL IN THE SEASHORE SAND

There was once a man who lived in a great city where, as every one knows, the spirit of "take" rules stronger than the spirit of "give." This man followed the ways of his time. He was very diligent in getting from the wealth of the city all that he could for his family. He spent many hours over the evening light figuring on his accounts in hopes he would find a way he could get more, but the many hours he spent in such figuring reaped as many hours of doubt and fear. For this man lived in a city where people were always afraid. They were afraid others would take from them all that they so diligently tried to take from each other. And he, like the other citizens of that city, went round and round within this fear like a squirrel on a wheel.

One day his wife, who was also very thrifty and never bought what would throw them into debt and so commit them to the other "takers" of the city, came to him and said: "While our children are small we should have a little car, but I have figured our income carefully and find we would need just a hundred dollars before we could with safety undertake to buy one."

Now the man wanted to do all that he could for his children, so it happened that, when his wife thus presented him their need, he caught a glimpse out through the cage of fear that held his city captive and answered her more wisely than he knew. "I'll tell you what we will do," he said. "When our little child with his tiny hands dug a well upon the seashore, was he afraid that the well would not be filled? No, but instead he sat down beside it and frail, but with faith, he waited for the ocean, miles wide and miles deep, to stir through and through to its deepest fathoms and fill it for him. We shall be as wise as the child."

But his wife said, "I do not understand."

And he found great difficulty in explaining to her, since it had but that moment come to him. But he said: "If we have a well, the great tides of God must fill it. If we have not a well but only think that we have, then there is nothing to be filled. It draws its fulfillment to itself inevitably. It becomes a great vortex, pulling to itself just the amount and kind to fill it, the exact fulfillment for the need, in right proportion, with no more and no less. It cannot be otherwise."

So firmly did the man hold to his new vision that he and his wife agreed to leave it entirely to God whether they should have their car by spring. Still one hundred dollars was needed before they dare venture. But the man did not lose faith. Instead he said to his wife, "Our child did not lose faith when he sat by his well on the seashore. Perhaps the tides did not come as soon as he had builded the well, but the tides came and he knew they would come. We shall have as much faith as he." And they waited.

Then through the mails came a letter which, when opened, dropped at their feet one hundred and eight dollars. They looked at each other in astonishment. When they turned to the letter which accompanied it they found that no fabulous person had sent it, but they themselves, twelve years previously, had *given it* to an endowment fund. Now, as the need which they had filled was no longer imperative, the tide had turned, their gift had come back to them when their need called. The man and the woman looked at each other, thinking the same thoughts. All they had taken had given them nothing. What they had given now returned to them made rich by their present need.

Thus the man came to know and it was borne out in his future dealings with his fellow men, that what he took profited him nothing, but all that he gave bore fruits with a thousand seeds, each seed to bear a many-branched tree which would in turn bear more fruit laden with more seeds, so that the abundance thus generated could never be reckoned.

When he came to know this he left off fearing and spent his evenings no more at mean figures. He thought no more of what he could take, for he had no need to take anything; for he gave so much and the body of those gifts bore such abundant fruit that his family seemed to live then on the shores of a great sea which bore up to them according to their need and never once after that failed them.

10

THE PARABLE OF THE OAK THAT DREW SUSTENANCE
FROM THE ELEMENTS

"Here I am," said a man, "getting along past the meridian of life, and have nothing to show for my efforts.

"All these years I have striven to give a true account of myself before God and my fellow man, and have failed. Having had the best preparation in college and professional school that money will buy, and having had ample opportunity to show my ability in at least three different lines of work, here I am left stranded high and dry, like a miserable piece of flotsam on life's wide sea. There seems to be no work for which I am adapted."

"Sit on the bench beside me," said his friend, "and look at this giant oak before us. See how it drinks through its leaves the same air that the little plum drinks in yonder. It draws nourishment through its roots from the same soil. The same rain blesses then with its showers, and the same sun shines its benediction down upon them both. From all these elements in nature the oak draws sustenance, just as does the plum. And yet the oak does not become a plum, nor the plum an oak. Each is governed by the inner law of its own being, which takes from each element exactly that which its own peculiar nature and genus demand, and rejects that which it cannot use. Look carefully, friend, at the oak—it is especially like unto you, for it, too, is late in arriving.

"You cannot, by taking thought, add one inch to your stature. But you can by being true to the law of your own being—even as the tree gives itself to the air and the sunshine in perfect trust to the great Father who governs all things, both the lilies and you—draw unto yourself exactly the opportunities, the environment, the friends that you need, and your success will be measured only by the dreams and desires which are rooted within your own integrated, unified self."

And the friend walked away, but the man still sat there and stared at the oak, until it became no longer a fancy or a dream, but a living fact—that the law which governed the oak also governed him, and that which was his could not ever escape him, and that which was not his could never really belong to him.

And days went on and a great quietness came into his soul. He could not understand it, because always before he had been unrestful at heart. Neither could his wife understand it, nor his friends. And then one day a man came to him with a wonderful offer which became the door to a career of true usefulness and happiness. And how and why it came he knew not, neither did his friends, nor did he ever meet anyone who could tell him. But as he passed the oak tree one day, he suddenly knew why it had come to him. For he knew that within the oak there was a power which was continually creating that which its inner nature craved from the silent elements without. And great calmness henceforth stayed with that man, a calmness that to others seemed colossal when those about him seemed lost in inconsequential things.

11

THE PARABLE OF THE NOISY STATION
AND THE MEADOW BY THE BROOK

The man and the woman were on a train with their three children, waiting at a station before they could go on to their home from which they had been away the entire summer. The woman had met her difficulties bravely. The three children had been ill all the summer; new labors, unexpected problems, had come upon them until the tangle had become inextricable.

Then the man and the woman had sat down opposite each other, for they had come to the end of their endurance and now knew that they must come together to find some courage.

The man said: "We must change our inner consciousness. Something is the matter within, since the reflection is so distorted. We must put ourselves in order." They did not know clearly what the man meant by this. It was simply that despair made them humble and very simple, and the man said, "That is all that I know to do in our predicament." And the woman agreed with him. So they had set about it together.

And no sooner had they done it than everything began to change. Letters came postponing important meetings which had been pressing upon the man; others bearing good tidings telling of problems which they had anticipated meeting in the future but that had now been settled for them. And finally, to their astonishment and much beyond what they had hoped, the children grew so strong and well that their very exuberance and vitality and good cheer seemed to bring good health to all within the home.

The man and woman pondered and wondered over what had happened to them.

Months had now passed and they were going on another journey. They sat in the great train shed in a metropolitan Union Station. The heat about them was stifling. Men were shouting at each other, children were crying. Thick smoke moved slowly in the heated air. They heard the shrieking whistles and the movement of the steel trains. Hot, tired people crowded down the aisles, trying to get into the next coach. All this noise, dirt, and ugliness were pressing down upon them like a nightmare, a darkening pall. They wished that this dirty, noisy station were not there, that they might be put into green meadows out under the sky.

Their wish had no sooner been expressed than a strange thing happened. The train next to them began to move. All the trains in the station seemed to be moving. The station itself seemed to be mounted on wheels, moving past them and speeding away. Everything moved. Suddenly the open sky came rushing in, the green meadows passed them, and they smelled the sweet grasses. That which they had wished for had come. Did their wish move away the unhappy surroundings? It had merely synchronized with the schedule of the Master Engineer up ahead, always carrying one from stifling quarters out into the open country, from places of want to places of abundance, from stations of ugliness to meadows of beauty and love and joy. For the schedule that the train of our inner consciousness goes by is a schedule not made by hands, but is made of the spirit, eternally woven of God's eternal purposes, a schedule which, if followed, will never bring destruction, but always carries those by the right track to greatness, joy, and beauty.

"And now," said the man, "we still do not know if the trouble moved away from us, or if we moved away from the trouble."

"What does that matter," asked the woman, "just so long as we know by turning to God we may be eternally separated from all that is bad and be eternally united with all that is good? But," she added, with sudden assurance, "I did not have to wait until this happened to find out that merely to change the inner consciousness can change the aspect of the entire world outside.''

"And when did you find it out?'' asked the man, looking at her.

And she answered him, shyly, "When I first loved
you.''

And the man was astonished and very happy.

12

THE PARABLE OF THE RAINDROP THAT GAVE ITSELF
' TO THE SUN

A wise man was sitting by the turn in the road when a
man all bowed down with troubles came and sat down at
his feet.

"You are in trouble,'' said the wise man. "I can see it in
your face and by the way you walk. If it will bring release
to your captive soul, tell me what it is that besets you.
Don't be afraid to speak.''

The man just sat in the road, stared hard at the
ground, and replied, "But my story is such a long story
and my troubles are even like the grains of sand which lie
on the sides of this pathway. I am without money and
without work and without friends. Things have come to
such a muddle that no one possibly could unravel them.
What more need I say?''

"My friend,'' replied the wise man, "there is no need
to tell me more. There is one way of escape which, if you
find it, will be just as effective whether your troubles are
one or legion.''

"But,'' interrupted the man, "you do not understand.
There is something in my situation which complicates it.
It is founded on misunderstandings and on mistakes and
on sin.''

"Little does it matter,'' said the wise man, "what it is

founded on, for the way I shall show you will be as easy to travel as the unresisting air, and as sure as the passage of light. True, there will be a yoke that you must bear and a burden that you must carry, but the yoke will be easy and the burden will be light."

"Show me the way," said the man, "for I am weak and heavy laden, and if I go much farther along the road I am traveling I shall drop in the dust, and there will be no one who will mourn me."

"Do you see that little mud puddle over there by the side of the road?" said the wise man. "In that puddle are drops of water that were once just as clear and pure as the water which is carried in yonder cloud above. The little raindrops in that puddle are crying out for escape and what will you do to help them? Will you tell them to strive and struggle? No. The more they struggle, the more the water will be disturbed and the more sediment will arise from the bottom. Will you put an antiseptic or purifying solution in the water to cleanse it of its germs? That would only exchange one form of impurity for another. Will you put your hand in the puddle and press down the mud and try to confine it tightly to the bottom and to the sides? No, that would not bring release. There is only one way, and that way is always open. You will tell the drops of water to turn away from the sediment that lies at the bottom and look toward the sun. You will tell them to give themselves unresistingly to the drawing power of the sun's rays. Then, no matter how much or how little are the impurities in the pool, how black or how thick the mud, the escape is easy and the effort required is light. For remember this, that no matter how your pathways are hindered and blocked here below, the way that leads upward is always clear and free and open."

And the man who was seated by the road ceased to stare down at the dirt, but turned his face upward and with eyes all shining, looked full and clear into the eyes of the wise man, and in those eyes he saw nothing but love, for the wise man looked upon him and had compassion upon him. "Now," he said, "I know what you meant when you said to look toward the light."

And he went on his way and the wise man never saw him again, but there came back, in the years to come, many rumors from a far, far city of a man who arrived one night in rags, but with a face that shone like the sun. And everything that came to that man brought him good fortune, and all those who became associated with him received good fortune as well. For no one henceforth could associate with him without catching something of the spirit which he carried in his soul. And that spirit was like the spirit of one who has risen in the morning and is beholding the sun.